The Library Room

Locust Alley

Screen Porch

Garden Shed

Main Stair Hall

pantry

Kitchen

Cooking

Side Entrance

Main Entrance Hall

Kitchen Bedroom

Dan's Office

Library House

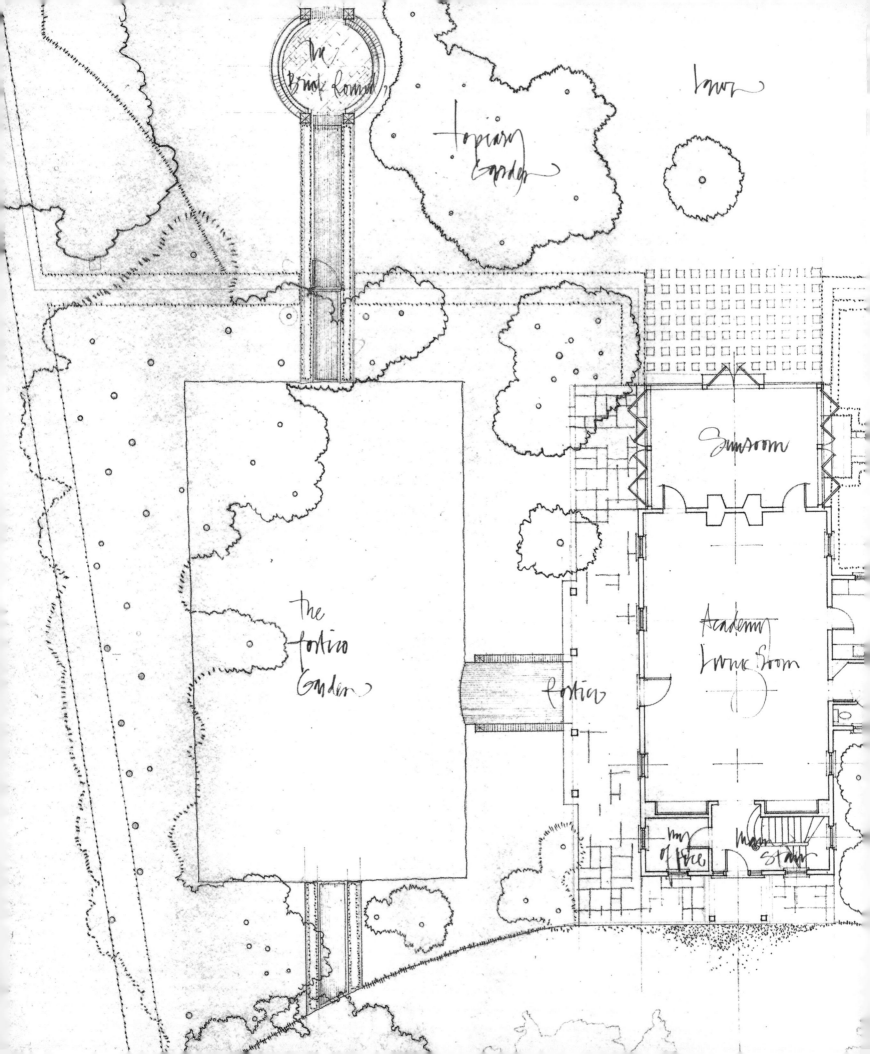

THOMAS O'BRIEN
LIBRARY HOUSE

THOMAS O'BRIEN LIBRARY HOUSE

Written with Lisa Light

Photography by Francesco Lagnese

Abrams, New York

For Dan

"Te enim vidi somnium.
Semper te amo."

Contents

Imagining a House

In so much of what I do, I'm inspired to make old things new again. Or, more specifically, to make new things that feel as though they come from some other, older time, things with an echoing sense of familiarity. I've always been one for whom history and stories matter, and I like to put history to use. I'm interested in homes and the objects in them that are designed to work for the present; they come from somewhere elegant and true, yet they take you somewhere unexpected and new. This isn't nostalgia as much as it is a grounding in the really perfect design qualities of so many useful things, tempered and refined over generations, that we can reinterpret, reinvent, or elaborate on, but which we can never quite let go of. To me, this is the definition of what's classic.

And beyond traditional or modern, that's my aim in everything I create, certainly in my interiors, and on special occasions, in the crafting of a house in every detail from the ground up: to capture time and bend it to the present.

This is how I began with the project that my husband, Dan, and I have come to call the Library House: a guesthouse and design studio situated in a series of gardens, next door to our home on Long Island known as the Academy. It started with the dream of a garden, then expanded to the dream of a house. I had the good fortune to build both, cultivated from the ground up, over about six years. Now it's a place where we recharge, create, and work—where we can invite clients and colleagues, families and friends to visit and see a way of living. It's an elegant, warm home for entertaining, equipped in the way that fine family houses were built for gatherings long ago. The furnishings and decoration

The walled garden at dawn, looking back toward the library room.

are abundant—happily layered, garden-infused, handmade, and determinedly pretty, a natural antidote to the twenty-first-century diet of technology and aesthetic spareness. There is a central kitchen for both formal and informal dining that draws on wonderful old kitchen traditions. It is also set up like a modern loft—for the lunches and dinners and cooking together that are a core part of each day, happening right in the midst of this very large, artistic room, the library. And of course, this is a place where we spend as much time outdoors as we do indoors.

This book is the story of imagining that house, and ultimately, how we now enjoy living here. It's about giving form to favorite ideas that I'd been thinking about for many years, from the outside in—the revival of a more formal architectural character that is getting ever harder to preserve and build today (the mouldings, millwork, cabinetry; the detail of the façades; the many stairways and fireplaces; the opportunity to create a set of most special bathrooms and an inventive kitchen). In fact, the design and construction of both the house and the gardens have everything to do with learning and time, with preserving craft, and with adding to history rather than discarding it. The whole home is an echo of the past; the experience of an eccentric, charming, rambling, generational, hand-built old home, translated into the brand-new invention that it is, all from the time of now.

And from the inside out—rooms designed and fitted around cherished pieces of furniture and favorite routines, the older and practical rhythms of caretaking at home that I've always loved. The keeping rooms and cabinets holding all kinds of housewares, linens, silver, dishes, glass and crystal; the fact of a full library, in and of itself. Collections of art, objects, and treasures, the meaningful finds and furniture that Dan and I discovered in our travels. Ever-present flowers, rich patterns and colors, signaling life and joy. The studio and storehouse of many of the products that I've designed, and all kinds of antique ingredients that inspire new ones. Books and objects at the ready to inform, as we design new projects and think on ideas to come.

Like anyone assembling and saving things over time for their ideal home, I gathered my own constellation of all these things over decades. Putting together a collection is not an overnight endeavor. It is a personal history. One begins to see themes and variations and adds to the collection so that there are groupings and stories. Yet in my life as a designer, much of this history had no place to settle for many, many years. Parts and pieces had been sequestered in storage spaces and relegated to temporary perches in my homes and at my company, Aero, in New York, quietly waiting.

Much like a garden, really, the house grew up and around these special things as much as they grew into it.

And so the whole project is truly alive, assimilated and added to as new things are discovered. We are surrounded by the touchstones that we look to all the time in the work we do and the way we live. And they become new things, because we use them now. All have finally found their home here.

From the time I was a small boy, I've been interested in people's homes. I always wanted to ask about furniture and art, or anything that was an heirloom. I think this is because I'm naturally curious about how such things reflect the reality and the interests of the people who live there, their particular history. I'm always drawn to the details, how things were made, how they age and last, how they show the hand and the creativity of some talented person in designs both fine and simple. That creativity, fine and simple, is for me the best and most authentic outcome of any design process—the individual choices; the practical needs that anchor a place or an object in real life; and the lens of other favorite houses, gardens, styles, arts, that all reveal what someone's dreams are.

These are the houses I've always most admired, from any period. They make the old into something new. They make the new feel that it's always been there. They make something classic that will last.

I wanted to build a place like that, where everything is personal, everything has a story, everything is to be used and appreciated and no detail is spared. So, I'd like to invite you to take a walk through the Library with me. And if the house looks like it's always been here, well, that's the magic that I'm always working toward. That's what I most wish to make for people. To create something that's real and magical at the same time. And the trick of that turns out to be everything.

At the Front of
the House

On this quiet village lane by the sea, the Library House presents itself in much the historical spirit of the Academy next door. It appears to be a relatively compact, traditional, 1830s-style, shingled country house, set among old trees and gardens. Yet a larger building is fitted behind this imagined oldest front part of the house, with a white-painted, neoclassical brick wing, conjured as the kind of expansion that would have been added in the 1920s. The building feels as if it has been here and been added onto over many generations, but it is all new—a newly made old house.

A New, Old Building

In my experience with both old and modern houses, I'm fascinated with the honest, perennial appetite for renovation and home improvement that are ingrained in American life. It's a process I work on often for my clients. It begins with a mix of needs and hopes—for more space, for a better kitchen, for more light or modern amenities. And then opportunity arises—whether the resources and right time for a gut rebuilding coincide, or the apartment next door becomes available to break through to, or a property next door comes up for sale . . .

Many, or even most, of these kinds of stories have intriguing preceding chapters. The story of the Library starts back in the 1920s, when one could see clear down to the Great South Bay from the Academy, across an open field. The original neoclassical, nineteenth-century building with the refined belfry had been the first schoolhouse in the Long Island village of Bellport. A poet named Anne Lloyd had moved the school down the lane to its current site closer to the water, perched on a small bluff twenty-five or thirty feet above sea level, with a line of lovely old oak trees along the edge

ABOVE: The Library in winter.

PREVIOUS PAGES: The front of the house was designed with windows paired and positioned in various ways, with a setback wing, which one sees in many early New England homes. All of the shutters, the front door, and the fanlight are painted in classic Litchfield Green, a favorite, darkest, not-quite-black green that I love for its crisp, graphic, and authentic feeling.

of the field and a beautiful, large copper beech tree that dated to the colonial mid-1700s. There she graciously converted the school into a home, added on a wing, and moved in. That open field next door is where the walled garden of the Library sits today.

Generations later, in my time living at the Academy, I'd filled the house with books and artifacts that I was saving: for a number of years, the small middle bedroom upstairs was called the treasure room, overflowing with accessories and art. I was beginning to want to do something more. And with all these collections, I increasingly needed a studio and design library where I could work outside of the city.

Then about three years before Dan and I met, the small 1950s colonial ranch house next door to the Academy went up for sale. This house had been built on a parcel carved out of Anne Lloyd's original property, where that open field had been. I took the leap; I bought the house and started planning.

With the new space next door, I first wanted more than anything to build a traditional English walled garden. I generally wanted to erase the sense of where the property line was and to let the gardens merge. There were special old trees here to protect: a flowering cherry, an old dogwood, a uniquely tall old apple tree, a huge sprawling yew, with the copper beech at the center of it all. I started by putting in a large raised vegetable garden at the back of the house because I knew that, during the years of construction, it would shelter the trees that would eventually become part of the walled garden.

With the building itself, the design process occurred in waves. As with many renovations, everything I wanted to do had to fit into the existing site and there were rigorous restrictions on how I could use the lot. I needed to maintain the original footprint and a percentage of the same walls and partitions in the ranch house's original shape. I found a way to build up and

create a second story, and expand as much as I absolutely could. I resolved how the studio would go below without losing light. In the end, the house ended up with seven stairwells.

Like the walled garden, a new grand room was a first imagining in my sketches—a library of books and art, with all the dinnerware, lighting, textiles, and furniture that wanted to come together in one place. I envisioned a more composed house around this large library, with

Elcy and Totie in the library room.

13

more traditional settings and room for guests. And as the project went on, and then Dan and I began building our life together, we did need more spacious bedrooms and bathrooms for visitors and family. Likewise, much as we love our home kitchen at the Academy, we needed and imagined more space, like the type of social kitchen that I often design for my clients.

What grew out of this process was a new, old house of the kind I'd always wanted to build. As a sister building on the property, this is the dressier, more tailored counterpart to the casual lightness and the uncommon schoolhouse history of the Academy. This house is about the feel and lushness of the garden, in which it literally sits, whereas the Academy is more a home by the sea. And this house references a more classical sphere of design, architecture, and gardens, more European in many ways, which I love and which actually informs my modern work.

There are modern ideas here, too, in the big library room with its 14.5-foot-high ceilings, scaled like both of the urban, vintage lofts in Soho that my store Aero has occupied. Yet the room feels more intimate because of

the big staircase down to the studio in the middle of it. The kitchen, then, also bridges the front of the house to the library wing and the tall staircase up to a master suite. Each decision connected to the next. From the beginning I wanted this all to feel as if it had evolved over a century or two, and that the different floor levels were purposeful. The whole house flows up and down at the same time.

All of this is now fitted in and behind what would have been the historic front façade of the oldest, 1830s-style part of the house. The Library presents to the street in much that spirit, a vernacular nineteenth-century, shingled country home, with a pedimented front door and a dappled, tree-filled yard.

Because of the variances and constraints I was working within, the house couldn't help developing without this kind of secret, meandering illogic of time. The work of the connecting and problem-solving in the architecture—truly the great fun of it, for me—was combining all the ideas and spaces that I wanted to coexist here, until all the pieces fit together and inside the shape of what had been.

ABOVE: A view of the Library from the Academy, across the kitchen garden.

OPPOSITE: At the open porch of the Library side door, this marble-topped
iron table is the resting spot of things going back and forth between the houses.

Through the Entrance Hall

The entrance hall establishes the tone for the house in both design and architecture. It is dark, European, and classical, with large-scale mouldings and paneled doors. Like a small gallery, it contains art and furniture; it is a place not only to enter, but also to slow down. From here, the house unfolds at a winding pace, moving through transitions, turning corners, arriving at landings, and traveling up and down stairs to discover where you are. And we find the library at the last turn of it all.

Arriving

In reconfiguring the front quarters of the new house, I wanted to have a formal entry hall take the place of the shallow foyer that had originally opened onto the ranch house's living room. As the main entrance from the street and for guests, the hall also needed to be the buffer between the two parallel front rooms on either side of it, which we love and use so much: Dan's office to the left, and the ground-floor kitchen bedroom to the right.

The transition from the American, casual spirit of the Academy next door to the more classical soul here begins in the architectural detail—and in the effect of this type of quite English hall, altogether. This was especially true and necessary given that the main staircase occurs in the back of the house, not at the front. Yet the scale in the architecture is also quite modern. With the room's high ceilings, the entry hall doors are the most formal and tall in the house, and they have the most striking, oversize casings. For these doors I designed strong, boldly carved mouldings in the style of English, pre-Georgian, Wren-period millwork, based on examples from a favorite 1920s reference book that I've used for years to create details. I always hunt for old books like this of period architectural studies that include sheets of mouldings, skirtings, door panels, dado rails, and so on. This is how generations of designers used to study and adapt examples from past traditions, and it's always a valuable resource to me still to use these books.

The raised paneling on the doors themselves is actually meant to be in more of a French style than doors I've designed in projects in the past—the elongated scale and subtle shaping is more Continental than American or English in feeling. I intentionally looked more to Europe for these details, to create the different elegance I wanted here. And it was part of the pleasure of this invention, throughout the house and in so many of the projects I do, to bring features together that wouldn't have necessarily coexisted in the past, but which feel very nice and right together in the present. Thus, I wanted to include a classic Dutch door before the pair of French doors that sections off the first vestibule, with its velvet-draped coat closets. The relaxed and formal together—this is one way that design can move beyond reproduction into something original that still has historical roots.

I focus a good deal on doors in all my projects and with my clients, because they do as much as anything to set the order of a house. In the entry hall these are the first order of doors in their detail and size. They're also identified by their color as the darkest doors, in a color scheme that moves from deep, cool, blueish grey to paler grey doors and trim colors throughout the house. I wanted to recall the black doors at the Academy, which have been a staple I've loved using over the years, but also do something softer and more restful in this house, which could again feel more chic and more formal.

As with the grey color palette, I wanted to find rich material for the floors that could be used to unify various areas of the house. I'd long been inspired by the

PREVIOUS PAGES: The tall nine-foot doors to the entrance hall create an intimate vestibule at the front door. I found the pair of unusually matched, American neoclassical, white-painted urns set on green-painted pedestals in Hudson, New York; such classic American colors. Elcy Jones and Totie O'Hara are the real commanders of the house.

dark floors at Austin Val Verde in Montecito, California, and I found a lightly tumbled black marble tile that I applied here and then in various different patterns throughout the passageways and the studio downstairs. Elsewhere, the house has dark oak floors; in fact, it's only the library room in this house that has light-stained floors, like those next door or in my city apartment. Ingredients of modern, pale, loftlike rooms do echo here, but only in the context of this richer, enigmatic palette.

That has been a fun mix to create, something much more elusive and Old World in character that can feel warm and surprising in contemporary life.

One thing I've always liked so much about Old World and especially English houses is the lightest way with which people live with mixes of antiques, furniture, and art. One sees this in the prolific inclusion of other cultures, Japanese and Chinese and Indian pieces, as well. For me, it's not so much the status that's important as it is that each thing, each carving, frame, spoon, glass, fabric, carpet, is made with such wonderful knowledge and care. I believe that kind of beauty is an ingredient that can contribute to a happier life.

Another inspiration here is the idea that collections and furniture are meant to be comfortable, enjoyed,

occupied, and not intimidating, no matter their provenance. So even in the entry hall, with its enveloping colors, sparkling light, and special furniture, we're inviting people to feel at ease with antiques and with layers. Beauty and comfort are made equals in every detail of the house.

I upholstered a circa 1810 American mahogany and marble Empire sofa in shimmering, embroidered Indian silk. Small gilded frames surround a midcentury, theatrical, nocturne painting with an aqueduct floating in the night sky. The gold frames were traditionally made to hold ceramic medallions or miniature paintings, but I love them as sculptural forms against the dark walls.

Resting in the reflection of an eighteenth-century, New York Federal gilt mirror is a special portrait of Jack Kerouac in Morocco, taken and inscribed by Allen Ginsberg. The photograph was a birthday gift to me from Dan. The primary doors in the entrance hall are painted Raccoon Fur by Benjamin Moore. The neoclassical revival bronze lantern is one of a pair in the hall, made in the 1920s.

The American mahogany, George II bow-front desk dates to 1760 and came to auction from the collection of the Metropolitan Museum of Art. It was one of the last few antiques we found for the house. The very intriguing, hand-crossed Degas self-portrait is placed in a wonderful antique gilt frame from Gill & Lagodich, the talented archival museum framers. All the roses are from the garden, of old varieties that date from the 1820s and later. Dan and I found the pair of petite, limed oak lamps with linen shades in London.

Light pours into the entrance hall from the front yard. A defining element of the hall's decoration is the pair of large, unusually dark 1940s scenic paintings on panels, in shades of black, inky blue, and brown, which were originally made as theatrical backdrops. I found them at one of my favorite antique dealers in New York and I loved their vaguely classical character, with a temple in one and the aqueduct with tiny ships in the other. They fit beautifully between the doorways. In the front vestibule, we created open closets covered with tall curtains of brown cotton velvet.

Alongside the House Next Door

From the very beginning, when I imagined the new Library, it was so important to link this house to the Academy next door. Always a first idea in the design was to position the side entrance to face the kitchen door of the Academy, so that you could see directly from one kitchen into the other. This is also the place where the two parts of the new house are joined: the shingled "original" house and the white brick wing that contains the library, the kitchen, and the main stair hall. The garden allée erases the long property line between the houses even more and brings the whole world here together.

The Side Entrance

I'm always intrigued by the way old houses show their seams and generations, when the additions, wings, and architectural styles of different eras are visible and not stripped away. Oftentimes these pieces fit together like a puzzle, where each resolution is added to the one before, making for some of the more rambling and most enchanting buildings that feel magical to be in. I love old houses that surprise in this way—rooms with windows that look onto other indoor rooms; halls that end in an unexpected view; later, newer entrances into larger spaces. You can feel the accumulation of time in all these twists and turns.

This is how I imagined the Library House would have evolved. And for this project I could invent the addition I'd always wanted to build, a classic white brick wing with a portico and a screened-in porch, framed along the side and between the two houses by a vintage garden allée of trees. In the interior, after the dark, English richness of the front hall, this section of the house would open up, be more light and airy, more connected to the gardens.

There is an ease that comes out of this symmetry, as we use this entrance most to go back and forth between the two houses. And they do become part of the same world in an intuitive way thanks to that fundamental alignment.

In designing this side of the building and the spaces that open up from this entrance point, I could then organize the positioning of every window, door, and room, in ways that don't always look the same outside to inside. I could add the brick wing and staircase hall I'd always imagined, with an exterior that has several graduated sections, each with its own architectural interest, along the view we see from the Academy and the length that takes us to the gardens behind the house. This was part of the fun. The figuring was in how to use this elegant long axis of the house and the varied rooms and entrances on its perimeter to move us inside and back outside to the garden, to present a beautiful staircase, and then, to eventually reveal the main library room.

One of the tricks of the plan for the house is the slight tiering of levels on the main floor where one goes up a few steps to get to the kitchen. The side entrance is the knuckle of the hallways and doorways that lead into the body of the house—bringing you up to the kitchen, aside to the main staircase nested toward the back of the house, and in the other direction, to the front hall and Dan's office. This would be an unusual

ABOVE: The Irish settee at the entrance. For years this basket always sat at every entrance to my furniture showrooms for Hickory Chair.

PREVIOUS PAGES: The girls like to travel the brick walkway between the Academy kitchen and the side entrance of the Library, and wait for us on the steps. This offset, scrolled lever handle is an elegant favorite of mine, and so convenient, with hands full as we go back and forth between the houses.

configuration for a more traditional early twentieth-century estate house, where a principal staircase would occur at the front, but it behaves just as an extension would in a small house of an earlier time.

Rather than feeling haphazard, these passages are unified by the continuation of the black marble floors from the front hall and—importantly in this lighter section of the building—by elegant, slender raised paneling on the walls and shallow column casings around the doors that I adapted from a favorite long-kept image of a classic vintage apartment in Rome. I do love what raised paneling can do to give character to any space, and this is a specific design I'd admired and wanted to use for some time. There had even been a modest bit of framed paneling in my first rental apartment in New York City, when I was just starting out, and it made all the difference from flat walls. So, this has always been a convention that I turn to and use in many projects. Thoughtful paneling and millwork of this kind can do more than any other architectural feature to make a family out of disparate spaces that have different dimensions and ceiling heights.

At this junction, the side entrance hall is more than a passageway but less formal than the main entrance hall. It is a favorite stopping point in and out of the house, and a dedicated space for certain things in our collection.

Here I was able to place the very tall, special Tiffany grandfather clock that I'd been keeping in the conference room at Aero. And I brought out the original, delicate, antique chinoiserie vitrine cabinet from when I first opened the gallery at Aero over twenty-five years ago. It is a one-and-only piece that I never sold, which had been hidden away in storage for years. At Aero it had always been the place for the special collections and small things that

needed to be protected behind glass. Here, it becomes a library unto itself that we get to look at every time we come in the house, with pieces of Greek and Roman glass and terra-cotta mixed together with other finds and totems, vintage and new.

There is a direct alignment between the Academy kitchen entrance and the side entrance here. We can see from one house into the other, and one kitchen into the other. The protected kitchen garden is beyond the hedge. I found the whimsical French garden lions at an antique shop nearby, and placed the pair here. They've never moved.

This porch around the side entrance is based on an Edwin Lutyens house that I loved, which gave me the idea of creating an open-air window on one side. We built a low Dutch door for the dogs, one of the many little corrals to keep them in as we are moving and unloading things. On winter days I gather kindling wood in this indoor-outdoor mudroom of sorts. The Italian marble figure is from 1820, from an old garden in Hudson, New York.

OPPOSITE: I always had in mind to place this beautiful, early nineteenth-century Audubon print of an American crow inside the vestibule. It is dated 1833 and charmed me because that is the year the Academy was built, and this was meant to be the first thing inside the door here, connecting the two houses. The antique iron sculpture is after the Farnese Hercules in Naples. It is American, from Troy Ironworks in upstate New York. In the nineteenth century, it was customary for iron foundries to make these classical figures once a year as a celebratory object. The hand-lettered alphabet is English and Georgian, and another nod to the schoolhouse next door. The special walking stick is Iroquois.

To the kitchen and the main stairs. From the side entrance we step up a few stairs to the kitchen, which overlooks the library room. Walking into the house, to the left is the passageway to the main stair hall with its very tall, paired windows. The lowered ceiling in the threshold is where the first landing crosses the stairs, into an art room that leads to the balcony of the library room: each section of the house is connected in ways that are both visible and hidden. The variations of panels and heights are indicators of this building that grew over time. Looking from the kitchen back to the side entrance, Dan's office and the front entrance hall are to the left; the main stair hall is to the right. A set of Georgian bells over the side entrance rings whenever the door moves. It's a tradition that started one Christmas with bells on the doors over at the Academy, and is meant to keep ghosts away.

Treasures in the glass cabinet. The chinoiserie glass vitrine in the side entrance is home to special Roman, Greek, and Cycladic antiquities and especially glass, among other souvenirs and favorite pieces. Above: a Roman Diana in marble with Roman glass bottles; a pale green alabaster Cycladic chalice with an opalescent Murano glass vase, made especially for Aero by Seguso; a delicate Greek terra-cotta profile on an Italian tray, surrounded by grandfather clock winders; a pair of eyes drawn by Dan's grandmother, Hilde Sigal, along with a pair of bronze greyhound bookends from 1925. The set of Edwardian books on the top shelf came from a large collection of turn-of-the-century novels and books with beautiful covers and elegant typography. On the bottom shelf, this pair of Norwegian ceramic polar bears has stayed with me for decades. I found them in my early days in New York City.

Toward the main entrance hall and into Dan's office. Pride of place in this side entrance is given to the neoclassical Tiffany grandfather clock. This spot in the entry was designed for it, as it was really the only place in the house where it could fit. Our wonderful clock restorer Stanley Bitterman, who takes care of this piece for me, once told me, "The clock is the heart of a house, with its ever-constant ticking beat." This clock does have the most beautiful Westminster chime, which rings all day through the house, on the quarter hour. Since childhood I'd always wanted a fine grandfather clock; when I finally found this example at auction, it was the one. It lived for a time in the conference room at Aero; with its dark wood and high classical pediment, we used to call it the Confessional. Now I wind it each week on the day we go back into the city.

CLASSIC AND MODERN

There is always something that intrigues me about juxtaposing old and new things, and seeing what arises in the combination. In this time of modern furniture I am still taken with the most intricate and detailed antique pieces; I like to find the newness in them by placing all that ornament in a simple setting. I found this incredibly beautiful, early twentieth-century Irish settee at Christie's one year. I fully connected to it, being Irish myself and loving all the animal parts of it, with its elaborate dragon armrests and paw feet. I also loved the botanical leaf and ribbon details of the shapely backrests, with such exceptionally slender, fine, and romantic carving.

This piece had been updated with a tight upholstered seat, but in older nineteenth and early twentieth-century houses, the true tradition would have been to have a loose, buttoned cushion on top. In restoring the settee, I decided to return to that form and lean in to the exotic embellishment, with a rich crimson gaufraged velvet that is somehow, on that soft, loose cushion, inviting and casual to sit on.

With this deep color in the light and dark entrance, the settee needed a striking and equally colorful piece of modern art for balance. I've long been an admirer and collector of Irving Penn; this evocative, famous photograph of frozen cubes of fruits and vegetables was a special favorite that hung behind my desk at Aero for several years. Paired together with the chinoiserie cabinet, the collection in the side entrance runs the gamut from the dearest, ancient Roman and Greek things to this modern art, and the settee from the period when this house was imagined to have been built. All are classic in their own way; each one, I think, demonstrates something lasting about the world of beauty.

Frozen Food with String Beans, New York, 1977, dye-transfer print by Irving Penn. The mahogany Irish settee is early twentieth century. A collection of walking sticks is stored at the ready, their natural wood shapes a counterpart to the elaborate settee. A perfect, remarkably unbroken Greek terra-cotta handled cup rests in the glass cabinet against the bronze mirrored back with a chocolate-colored, Chinese cloisonné jar.

The Locust Allée

To me, gardens are so like architecture. They are outdoor rooms, the sum of many details to discover and relish up close. Yet at the same time, they are always about what you see in front of you, what you find at the end of a view.

Creating a flowing passage along the prominent Academy-facing side of this house gave me an opportunity to do several important things. First, I wanted to set up gardens here that would erase the long property line and help to put the two houses together, including the outbuildings between them—a small garden shed and the Academy garage looking over the Library. I needed a terraced walkway to connect to the front of the house, which would allow us to step down with the gentle grade of the property until we arrive at the sunken garden behind the library room. And I'd always wanted to create a beautiful allée of trees. This could happen naturally here because of the length of the building.

There were some key ingredients that were part of the designing of this allée. Pathways and paving are so important in a garden, and I wanted to use traditional red brick for this walkway. Creating bordered and patterned brickwork is like designing tile or flooring patterns; it's a wonderful place to add a sense of history and order. And the color was going to be so handsome with the white brick of the house, very classic, light and dark in combination. In fact, I'd seen and always remembered a wonderful image of Clark Gable in front of his home on his ranch in Encino, in California, a white brick colonial house with a redbrick terrace and steps. And there was another image I loved of a Georgian house in England that had a level of redbrick masonry below millwork. So this pair of references, both so elegant and iconic in their own ways, led me to the redbrick. I used it again in the window wells for the studio along the side of the house, for that contrast beneath the white.

Entering the allée from the front of the house. I call this the little silver garden.

For the trees, I knew all along that I wanted to use honey locusts in particular, for the lovely, wispy shape of their branches and their delicate leaves as they turn bright, beautiful yellow and scatter through the autumn, almost like flower petals. Locust trees always remind me of the streets of New York City and they are here as well in the village on old Bellport Lane. I hand-picked eight seedling trees, four on each side, that were the most willowy and branching that I could find.

With these features, the allée is one of the most crafted, subtly formal parts of the garden. Walking up and down it is a kind of processional. Practically, it is how we access many parts of the house. That natural formality especially matches the fine main entrance to the library itself, through the portico. Where the side entrance is for moving back and forth between houses, and especially kitchens, the portico is the proper, grand threshold into the library. It is an invention of forms that combines a set of favorite architectural details; the columned colonnade grew out of an image of an English house that I'd kept with me since my earliest days working for Ralph Lauren. The colonnade is

another one of the open-air spaces around this side of the house, which bridges my office in the far corner with the screen porch to the other side, and connects us directly to the garden.

The view back up the allée from the turn into the sunken garden. The notions of the allée and the gardens in general have a French feeling and inspiration in many ways. The most meaningful of these influences is from Giverny, where a carpet of nasturtiums covers the central garden path on the main allée in front of Monet's house. Dan and I loved visiting Giverny and I've always so admired the gardens there. I knew I wanted to have beds of nasturtiums here in that spirit. They are a constant that we look forward to each summer.

The path of the allée, from the front of the house to the back, unites the many variations and windowed outlooks in the façade that aren't entirely matched. The side entrance is a columned porchfront with a fully open window looking down the allée. The bluestone paving up the large full stone steps leads around to the front yard. Summersweet is planted throughout all the parts of this garden at the side entrance. It was growing plentifully here in this spot when I began the Library. So it was the most natural thing to divide the plants and put them in all the beds of the garden here. The summersweet always blooms in late July and August. It's one of the singular moments that ties this garden and the side entrance to the times of summer, with its deep, honeyed fragrance.

PREVIOUS PAGES: The allée in summer, planted with low beds of nasturtium. The portico entrance is to the left; the garage of the Academy and the small garden shed are to the right.

Seasons in the garden. The Academy garage in the snow is behind the picket fence that meanders between the houses. My own little garden around the shed is the one that no one plants in but me, with old roses and other botanicals that remind me of the small plot I tended as a boy in my grandparents' vegetable garden. We would collect special plants as we went to greenhouses or apple picking, and this space is filled with specimens and flowers, just like that old garden. Nasturtiums grow up through the slats of a Regency bench that Dan and I found in London.

Doorways and gates. Above, the portico entrance in winter; down toward the sunken garden; the portico entrance in summer; the main gate between the two houses and gardens. To the left, under the copper beech, the gate behind the garden house leads to the gardener's work area.

It was very purposeful to make the progression toward the library room and the gardens behind the house all the more mysterious in terms of when additions might have happened and why. Yet all of the rooms open onto this shared view, with a soft, vintage, natural feeling that helps to pause modern time. As you step down, and away from the stress of modern life, you see that the Library is really resting in the middle of the garden in every way.

AT THE END OF THE VIEW

One priority that I set early on was to obscure what happened at the end of the allée so that you couldn't quite see beyond it—the end point of a view.

About a year into designing the house, I was at a favorite large tree nursery and discovered a very beautiful, huge, mature hinoki cypress tree, way far off in a field, alone and a bit forgotten. I thought it would be the perfect thing to position as the focus at the end of the allée, and I bought it right then.

The tree continued to wait in that field for several years, until the foundation to the house was in, the footing of the brick garden wall was finished, and the foundations were laid and done for the garden house. Planning a garden is all-encompassing work in this way, in terms of staging construction and anticipating planting, especially with large trees that need to be sited long before they can be moved.

Finally, it was time to bring over the hinoki. With a mature tree, that's always quite an exciting production.

This was a big one to do, that required a twelve-ton truck and a team of handlers to take care of the moving and planting. But when it was in place, the tree looked as if it had been long established right where it was.

It is something to be so carefully imagined with very mature plants and trees, to create a new history that feels authentic in a garden. The hinoki sits now in the shelter of the copper beech, a beautiful image at the end of the allée. And it's turned out to be a very good thing to help nurture the tree by putting it in the shade of the copper beech. In the winter it is the evergreen when all the other leaves are down, the most magnificent old-growth tree in the garden.

From here, we turn to the back of the library and into the sunken garden. And the garden house is hidden among the trees, behind the hinoki. That sense of concealment makes the gardens at the end of this property feel very magical, and once you turn the corner, all the more discovered.

The beautiful hinoki cypress with the golden leaf canopy of the honey locusts, at the end of the allée in late summer.

The Two
Front Rooms

The two front rooms begin the first part of this house. Besides the library room itself, these are the rooms with the highest ceilings and the only ones with the very tall, paneled, blue-grey glossy doors. The black stone tile hallway winds between them, taking us from dark to lighter spaces as we move closer to the library room itself. From the thoughtful mixing of modern and traditional furnishings in Dan's office to the rich patterns and colors abounding in the kitchen bedroom, this pair of rooms offers a first glance at what is to come, and they're among the spaces that we live in the most.

Dan's Office

Dan's office occupies the northern front corner of the house, with light pouring in from a set of windows that look onto the Academy front yard next door. From the earliest planning stages of the house, this was always one of a few places where the Library would be connected to the Academy by a direct view. In its position nesting in that corner, the office does have wonderful northern and western exposures that are so quiet and restful—it's one of the sunniest and most private rooms in the whole house. Dan's choice of a favorite, soft, ethereal green on the walls adds to this beautiful light and brings his room into the outdoors in its own way.

As part of what would have been the original front façade of the house, I designed the windows wrapping around this corner to fit within the style of the other New England shingled houses in this region and village. I based the massing of the windows in particular on a favorite old house right down the street, with a set of three bay windows that I've always loved. This openness also reminds me somewhat of a captain's quarters on an old sailing ship—the "great cabin" that would span the stern with a bay of large, illuminating windows.

In both this office and across the hall in the kitchen bedroom, I wanted to create a strong presence with tall, deep window casings set with raised panels top and bottom. The floor-to-ceiling millwork that I designed is drawn in part from my own family history, when I was a small boy and my grandmother renovated her 1840s house in upstate New York. In order to make a large, more modern living room, she combined the two traditional front parlor rooms into one space, reinterpreted the millwork, and repainted everything in a serene, cool shade of blue-green that I've always loved. There were these very beautiful raised panels set below the windows. That room was so elegant and American, in her house of the same period, and in another small village just like this one. As I considered the front rooms here, it was charming to me that she'd had these same two kinds of rooms made into one.

Time and again, I've carried forward the memories of that house, and I've used the details in many design projects for clients and myself. It's a special place to me. My grandmother taught me so much about looking at design: how to appreciate history and notice the fine and careful details of things.

Those panel details certainly fit the style of this front section of the house. Because of the height of both rooms, I took the large, curved Wren mouldings from the front entry hall and used them like tall and elegant cabinetry around the windows and doors. And though the rooms are so different, this millwork makes them quite complete as a pair. It is as though they were built together and come from one moment in the

ABOVE: The artful and intricately folded pages of a French book create a paper sculpture.

PREVIOUS PAGES: Books abound in every room of the house. A basket tray with special mementos and books sits on a Japanese deco tea table in Dan's office. A vintage folding stool, fully upholstered in my citrine-colored Paolo fabric, holds more books in the kitchen bedroom.

time-line of this place. The only spaces aside from the front of the house where these mouldings repeat are in the large door casings in the library room and the very grand, wide proscenium casing that frames the opening of the kitchen rooms onto the library.

In Dan's office in particular, this paneling has the most dramatic effect, as it creates the frame around the whole large corner of the window bay itself. I also used the large Wren profile here as a bolection moulding to create a classical frame around the fireplace that goes all the way up to the ceiling.

For me, every fireplace, in any room, is essentially as important and central as any large cabinet or primary piece of furniture; but of course, it's part of the house itself. For this fireplace, the Wren moulding forms a total casing and includes a tall recessed panel that would traditionally hold a mirror or painting. Here Dan chose a very special and unique find from the collection of paintings I'd gathered through the years, an early twentieth-century Walt Kuhn portrait of a young circus performer. Choosing one painting to sit above a mantel makes it the most definitive and elevated artwork in a room, just as central as the fireplace. In this prominent place, the character in this portrait creates a certain presence for the whole office.

This is a real office and study where Dan is often to be found on the weekends, quietly and intently work-ing and drawing. Each piece of furniture and his collections are full of history; the room is a library unto itself. He's filled his space with art, literature, and design; pieces that reflect his love of music and cinema, and many things French and European, from the 1950s and earlier modern decades, that speak of his roots and cultural interests.

Many of Dan's design projects have a modern bent, but here in the country and for the weekends, he's

created this room with its pale, verdant green walls and peaceful light that is, for him, the softer, lighter, brighter companion to the library. It's mixed, classic, eclectic, chic. The room is itself a window onto so many of the things that intrigue him.

The view from the front entrance hall into Dan's office. The strand of Tibetan bells is on one of the front tall paired doors, an old-fashioned tradition in both of our houses so that we can hear the doors open with a chime.

We found Dan's Louis XVI-style desk at auction. It has a handsome, heavily patinated leather top that we both loved, which we had carefully restored and preserved. Mixing the modern with the antique, an original Noguchi table is nested underneath the desk on one side, and a very fine 1958 Arne Jacobsen Egg chair in black leather sits to the other in the window corner. The desk chair comes from a set of 1920s dining chairs originally belonging to Dan's great-grandparents, which we brought to the house and recovered in chocolate velvet. They have a magical, old Hollywood feeling, as if from a movie like *Sunset Boulevard*, a somewhat-Tudor, somewhat-Spanish sort of hybrid. The ivory porcelain lion was a gift from me. Dan is an August-born Leo.

Dan's office is filled with special modern and art deco items, and selections of my furniture and lighting from over the years. My Julien sofa with its modern, curved silhouette sits in the center of the room in inky, navy blue velvet, next to a simple, vintage deco tea table, now used as a coffee table, that we found in Kyoto.

Much of what is most dear to Dan in this room comes from his artist grandmother, Hilde Sigal. She is an extraordinary person and incredibly prolific: she's been a central force on who Dan is as a creative and adventurous soul. Hilde came to this country from Vienna in the 1930s as a young teenager. She has lived a full life of art and culture, continuously making all kinds of paintings, sculptures, and assemblages since she was a young woman.

Some of her work has come here from her wonderful, art-filled house. In the glass cabinet is an iconic, inflatable doll by Niki de Saint Phalle. On an old, unique Gothic chair is one of her figural plaster masks. Other art is personal here, too: the large hand portrait above the chair is my own handprint, photographed by our dear friend Gary Schneider.

Within this paneled fireplace design made of the front rooms' large Wren mouldings, the sole Walt Kuhn portrait becomes a character in the room. Employing the millwork in lieu of a formal mantel created the need for a mantel shelf. A slender smoked-glass shelf on nickel brackets, from my first Waterworks bath collection, was a quiet, simple solution. It holds cherished objects, including an enigmatic pair of Egyptian glass eye inlays, from the first century AD. They gaze across the room to the front hall, watching over everything.

Throughout the house I chose a European-style, buff-colored firebrick for the interior of the fireplaces. I love the color and the narrowness of these bricks and applied them in different herringbone and bordered patterns and interpretations in each room. Dan and I also shopped together in Paris for all of the fire tools and andirons and other decorative equipment that accompany each fireplace. Though they can often be overlooked or underestimated, these functional elements are so special, essential, and charming, like treasures for the making of a fire.

We each have places in the house with treasured gifts from each other as well as the most personal souvenirs, and this room is one for Dan. In the corner of the office, an original Olympic Games flag from 1932 in Los Angeles hangs above a neoclassical cabinet that we found together in London. The flag was a gift from me that I found in Venice Beach, of all places. More French and Parisian things assemble in a still life on the coffee table. The name of the book is so enchanting and perfect: *How Paris Amuses Itself*. Along with the Egyptian eyes on the mantel shelf, other Egyptian pieces filter through Dan's collection. I set the grouping of Egyptian Ptolemaic period beads for him in a beautiful gilded panel frame one Christmas.

With the artworks from Hilde, and my childhood memories that led to the architectural detail of these front rooms of the house, we truly have memories and histories that are blended together here. We've also both been incredibly fortunate to have deepest ties with our kind, talented, and imaginative grandmothers. As inspirations and teachers, they both showed us how to love beautiful things and to look at the world closely, through creative eyes.

Dan's Bathroom

Detailing and creating bathrooms is always one of my favorite parts of designing homes, from the architecture to the finishes and furnishings. In the Library, all of the bathrooms are rooted in a shared early-modern archetype. In my mind's eye they're part of the fantasy of the house, with a remembered luxury from a classic age of bath design that I think is still relevant today. That said, each bathroom does have its own special character. For Dan's bathroom I got to conjure a specific design that I'd always wanted to create, with cork walls and a mix of pale grey and white marble.

I had two long-held images featuring cork walls that I loved—one of an English bathroom and one of a men's haberdashery window lined in cork—both favorites from my early days in design. I paired the cork with pale grey veined Italian marble around the shower and for the window casings and baseboards. For the vanity top here and in several of the other bathrooms, I found a very intriguing, clean, white Greek marble. In all my years of visiting stoneyards, I don't recall anyone ever labeling a marble as Greek before I came across this milky, beautiful stone. With all of the classical elements in this house and our collections, this was such a fine, unusual alternative to the more common Carrara-type marbles so often used. And in my imagination I found it charming and symbolic that it was Greek.

Marble is certainly an ancient material—not to be overly obvious—but when I go to the marble yards, I'm looking for stone that has another echo of time in

it, a different kind of cultural memory. I want to find the stone that feels as though it comes from a place you've always wanted to visit, the romance of Claridge's in London in the 1920s, a glamorous movie from the 1950s, a classic 1930s New York marbled lobby. I much prefer material that has this solid, earnest, almost cinematic, backstory to it, which reminds me of being from somewhere before now.

I named the gentleman's chest of drawers the Dan Chest in one of my earlier furniture collections. It stands just outside the door to his bathroom. With its cork walls and crisp metalwork, this bathroom has a simple, masculine, deco spirit.

Fine metalwork can do a similar thing to marble in terms of creating a vintage sense of place. The detailed framing of the shower enclosure and mirror are hand-fabricated in nickel plate for a warmer, older glow. The fixtures in this bathroom are from my original Aero collection for Waterworks, along with a few special prototype hooks that also came from my very earliest bath accessory designs. The warmer grey Italian marble in the room forms a tailored casing around a narrow window. Cloth-taped wooden Venetian blinds are another favorite vintage ingredient that I've used over and over through the years. The olive brown towels are from my former home collection for Marshall Field's, out of the library of textiles we have here from years ago.

The Kitchen Bedroom

Wallpapered rooms are beautiful to me. And in the classic character of this house, with so many different ideas and antique collections coming together, Dan and I knew we wanted to have wallpaper and rich patterned walls featured here and there in the Library. This is really the one room where I've used patterned walls in such a prominent way.

The kitchen bedroom is quite a special spot. There is something about this whimsical and deeply comfortable room that even the most modern-leaning people always and instantly love when they first see it. And it's certainly one of the few places in our lives where we've done something so absolutely traditional and antique. The textiles and patterns are continuous, delicate, layered, without needing to match. The furniture is highly carved and ornamental. This room, like Dan's office, is pleasant and airy because of its ceiling height and tall, panelized windows. But there is something about the richness and the colors, the enchanting wallpaper and all the botanical motifs in the furnishings, that delights visitors. It is pretty—such a valuable thing, though in important ways, simple prettiness has become too easy to forget in modern life.

The bedroom sits a few steps down from the kitchen, in a secluded sitting room–style space that is like a jewel box. The central idea for the room was a rabbit-themed wallpaper that I'd always loved called

Shimo, from Brunschwig & Fils. I'd noticed it as a paper that Albert Hadley used many times. From the first, it was one of those things that I absolutely knew I'd find a way to use someday. The pattern of kimono-clad rabbits is so obviously witty and darling, with such a fanciful Japanese theme. And I am so fond of the elegant coloring, with the chic kraft paper background and red robes. To me, it is all the definition of charming.

And curiously enough, though we didn't pick the paper for this reason, rabbits have become a character in our life here. Especially when writing this book last year, and after fifteen years of living at the Academy with a rabbit or two in the spring, the property suddenly became overrun with the most sprightly and sweet-looking rabbits everywhere, from the spring throughout the summer. They have been a whole new challenge for the garden but they are adorable and seem to have made their home among us, eating everything.

We embraced the wallpaper here completely. In addition to the field of rabbits, a red geometric fretwork border is printed at the edges of the wallpaper roll; I trimmed the room in it everywhere it could be. It runs all along the base of the narrow crown moulding, up every one of the casings, along the baseboards, and all around the mantelpiece. Every edge that touches painted millwork has this fine little fretwork as an almost architectural detail.

A turned mahogany bracket is one of a pair on either side of the fireplace; Shimo wallpaper behind.

In the layer-upon-layer character of this room, it was natural to add even more imagery on top of the wallpaper. The Cy Twombly prints above the bed add a modern, abstract ingredient amid all the tradition. I love collecting art of all kinds, and though more of our photography and modern art is in the city, it's nice to have an older house where pieces like these don't need to only hang on a plain wall.

From the walls down to the floor, another ingredient that is so important in a room is the right carpet. The incredibly unique example here appealed to me immediately in this room that I was imagining with pattern on pattern. It depicts the abstracted motif of a woman known as hands-on-hips, a fertility symbol from old Mesopotamia. But the most unique thing about the carpet for me is that it's a beautiful, bright, mossy green—a very uncommon color in Persian carpets. I tend to search out carpets that are more brown and blue, as reds and oranges are so much more prevalent, but this green variation with other rich colors was even more unusual. The carpet was purposely chosen for this room and laid out early in the construction to see how it looked, specifically because it was these colors of the outdoors, for this house in the middle of the garden.

Perhaps it's that this lovely bedroom sits at the front of the house; perhaps it's the height, or the objects, or the warmth of the colors in the room. But it does seem as though there is a preferred room like this in every old house, in every old movie or beloved old hotel, all rolled into the feeling of this space. And so this is the room our little family is drawn to, where we usually sleep in the house and where the dogs especially want to settle in. We do most of our cooking now in the more designed and established kitchen in the Library, and after dinner, at the end of the evening, the dogs wander to the top of the steps into the room. Elcy, who is fifteen years old and the one in charge of us all,

demands to be carried in to the bedroom and put up on the bed. During all the winter months we have a fire every night, and it is so enveloping to be in the antique bed, with the dogs, looking over the footboard in front of us. It's all of another time, but still somehow of the present as well. Each night we still find ourselves saying how much we love being in this room.

A McKim, Mead & White oak table from the Low Library at Columbia University holds books and objects in the sunny northern corner of the house.

The special green wool of this handwoven carpet is made of natural dyes obtained from a combination of daisy flower and indigo. Daisy provides acidic yellow and then the yarn is dyed in indigo to create this green. The inside of the yarn retains a glowing yellow. I designed the Elizabeth rock crystal chandelier for Visual Comfort, with a burnished silver leaf finish. Above, the French terra-cotta abstract silhouette sculpture was a birthday gift from Dan.

This wonderful Shimo wallpaper from Brunschwig & Fils has been a design classic for decades. Like so many nostalgic things that manage to hold their originality, perhaps it's that these colorful drawings of kimono-clad rabbits still feel fresh. I think of the way that playful illustrations of a certain era can be so sophisticated and approachable at once—like the murals in Bemelmans Bar in the Carlyle in New York. That sense of refined innocence seems to surprise and captivate people who always immediately love this room—even those who are inclined to like more modern things.

OPPOSITE: This mantel is one of the few pieces from the original ranch house that I kept and repurposed. It came from the living room. The shelf holds a pair of Victorian, very special botanical herbarium fans with ferns, which were found in London. I've had the charming, very early cast iron tea caddy for years. The roses are from the garden, in a handpainted 1920s grasshopper cocktail glass.

Above the bed hangs a pair of Cy Twombly lithographs, circa 1980. The tall doors on either side of the bed lead to the front entrance hall and are painted the same rich, blue-grey Raccoon Fur. Draped over the bed, the very fine vintage red and pale blue linen throw is something I bought when I was a student at Cooper Union, so long ago in the world of Soho, when there were still antique stores on Broome Street. It was certainly an expensive thing to me then, but I had to have it and treasured it. It has always been a piece that I've kept visible and very near.

Sometimes, I also find primary pieces of furniture that feel right and necessary, with absolutely no place for them to go. I came across the pair of nineteenth-century American mahogany pineapple post beds many years ago in a favorite antique shop in upstate New York. I was drawn to them even then for the beautiful way that they are so finely proportioned, with such detailed carving in perfect, fully matched right and left reverse profiles. I bought them, even though I had no place for them and certainly had no wish to change any bed in any room at the time. I had no intention of selling them either; I was just determined to use them someday. For this house, bringing them together would give us an eight-post, rather than four-post, king-size bed. Part of collecting in this way is buying and keeping loved things until their time comes. I buy beds for rooms that don't exist yet, but you never know . . .

P atterns and garden colors. This room is one of the primary places in the house for traditional pattern-on-pattern layers of textiles, flowers, bedding, and art. I was especially taken with the Matisse needlework pillow, which I would guess came from a 1950s kit. I found it so charming that someone did the stitching in green instead of the typical Matisse blue. The pillow sits atop an Amish quilt and a Beacon blanket I've had since my Cooper Union days. The intricate Indian miniature paintings are a set of four. The colors of the carpet bring red and green into the room. The dahlias from the garden in a Georgian sprigware jug stand in front of an early giltwood mirror that we found in London. The bedding incorporates a mix of textiles from my original Marshall Field's home collection.

The small bathroom to this bedroom is one of my favorites, made in this vintage green, almost minty color. There was an image I loved of an English bathroom with a cork floor, a tub with a wallpapered front, and a beautiful armoire. Years ago, for the kitchen in my first little house, I had covered the interior of a glass-fronted cabinet with this lovely Sanderson pagoda wallpaper: I had one roll left over that I kept all this time, which was just enough for the tub front here and the interiors of the narrow linen closets in the bedroom. This room is really just a little paint and paper and magic. Picture rails hold art hung on ribbons, including charming buttons arranged in the shape of an anchor.

THE TULIP CHAIR

I have always been drawn to the underlying simplicity in seventeenth-century Jacobean furniture—the squared shapes look almost modern to me. Those simple forms were mixed with all kinds of expertly scrolled and foliate carving that reflected the low-country, Flemish and Dutch influences of the time, emphasizing nature. I've had a modest 1920s chair with these kinds of profiles since college, which I slipcovered in ecru twill; it now sits in one of the guest bedrooms in the Academy. And that chair has the same 1920s, old movie-era style as the squared shape of the set of Dan's grandparents' chairs in this house. But, I'd never bought any furniture of the original period before.

Then, a number of years ago, I came across this exceptional chair of the period, which was intact with its original embroidered fabric. When I found it, besides its earliness and fine carving, I was told that the importance of the chair lay in the fabric's depiction of tulips—the symbol of the Dutch Golden Age, and a portrait of what was, in fact, most modern and all the rage in its time. Tulips were imported to Holland from Turkey in the late sixteenth century and were rapidly naturalized and cultivated. With their deep, vibrant petal colors, the flowers were unlike any other plant known to Europe at that time.

To me, the back of the chair can even seem like a Dutch painting. In the square form of it, the timbered frame might seem rigid, but instead holds this graceful canvas, celebrating the unique marvel of tulips. I learned that the chair had been kept for many, many years in a very beautiful bedroom, in dim, low light that protected the embroidery. It was amazing that it had survived for centuries in such wonderful condition, even with areas of fading on the fabric that might themselves have been restorations a hundred years old or more. I so appreciated that someone had taken such perfect care of this piece for so long; a responsibility of the sort that I seem to take on and enjoy in particular.

When I first had the chair, it sat just inside the Academy living room, in a shaded and sheltered spot by the portico doors. As I started the Library, I thought that someday it would sit in the master bedroom here. But I realized it was really more about this special bedroom that was developing, with its colorful pattern-upon-pattern ideas and gracious antique character. It seemed certain that it belonged here, bringing the garden into the room, with its elegant tulips juxtaposed against the charming rabbits of the wallpaper and the green field of the carpet. And it was at home all at once: a gem visible from the entrance hallway, the first thing you see from this room, and one of the oldest period treasures at the front of the house.

By the dark Raccoon Fur door, at the entrance to the kitchen bedroom from the front hallway, the seventeenth-century needlework tulip chair sits against the Shimo wallpaper. The paper's red fretwork border trim runs along the door casings and follows the baseboard around the entire room.

I do love designing cabinetry and millwork. No space is wasted here: I hid useful, shallow linen closets in the deep paneling of the window well to the side of the fireplace. They are lined in the same chinoiserie wallpaper used in the bathroom.

OPPOSITE: The view through the house. The bedroom is set down a few steps from the kitchen. These are the steps that we carry Elcy down at night when we are ready to settle in here. With the door open, one can see from the very front northwest corner of the house all the way to the back southeast corner near my office in the library room, and on to the gardens.

The Main Stair Hall

After the rich pair of tall rooms that we live in so much in the front of the house, we come to the even taller space of the main stair hall. From the outside, this is where the white-painted brick section of the house that becomes the main wing of the whole Library begins. Inside, I needed to create a space in which a stair could climb to the second floor and a new bedroom suite up above. We pass through a low threshold in the hallway that goes under the stair landing, and then the stairs turn back above, opening up into this airy, high-windowed hall that is filled with garden light.

The Main Staircase

In developing the plan for the Library House, I was creating a sort of continuing history that connected the major architectural parts of the building. Each set of details that gave finesse and shape to those parts had its own even deeper history, as I thought about when certain small pieces might have been added, or if they were clues to something that had been there before.

The stair hall is one of these parts. From both the outside and the inside of the house, it is the first segment of the white brick wing that leads to the library room and all that would have been in this imagined addition to what we think of as the older, shingled front section. When I was designing it, I first needed to invent two stories of height and head room in order to create a tall staircase up to a second floor that didn't exist in the original ranch house on the property. When I was thinking this through, I also knew I wanted a balustraded balcony along the library room, so I had to find a landing—a pause—that would take us up to a secret passage and into these two parts of the house that are joined. One part of the staircase goes up; one goes through a hidden door into this structure where the library room exists, and onto the long balcony. Each step revealed the solution for the next step—more details, more history, more of the intricacies that lead off of the stairs into these extra hidden spaces and charming detours.

So, in the making of these generations of the house, this staircase served multiple roles. And, because the stairs themselves had to turn back around toward the front of the house, they created the structure of a hallway that opens up into a bright, high, window-filled tower. The release into this tall, airy space at the end of the hallway is one of the emotional surprises and visual shifts in the house, from dark to light, low to high, that was so purposefully and carefully constructed.

In plan and in relationship to the whole property, this tower structure was also designed to sit directly across from our sunroom at the Academy. There is a certain kindred spirit in the way we see and use these sunny spaces that adds to the connection between the houses. The two structures are paired in visible ways, both having flat roofs with balustrades above. Yet relative to the simple neoclassical lines of the sunroom, the stair tower at the Library House is finer and taller. The balustrade here has raised panels in it, as well as a raised panel that is incorporated into one of the high windows where the staircase inside travels past it. The hall is unique along the façade for its series of tall, slender windows with smaller second-tier windows above, a classical Palladian idea that I wanted to translate in a very quiet way. And more than almost any other place in the whole Library House, what you see from the outside tells you exactly what the inside space is. A staircase is contained within.

In my ongoing imagining of these details, the stair hall is also one of those elusive spaces that I like to think of as having a preexisting past. With the quixotic

PREVIOUS PAGES: Looking from the library room into the main stair hall, with its tall windows and eastern light pouring in from the allée. Among my collection of American Impressionist landscapes and portraits that line the stair, one treasure that sits beneath the Venetian mirror is *Village at Dusk*, painted in the north of France by Louis Comfort Tiffany. The heirloom and wild roses are the oldest of the varietals in the garden, from the 1820s and 1830s.

way that the stair cuts across the windows, the hall does seem as if it might have been an even earlier room with tall windows in it, that became reworked as a staircase later on. Besides the desire to create this pair of tall windows on the outside, one of the purposes of both the exterior and interior is that I knew I would be able to have a window for a powder room tucked away below the stair. And this was a charming and perfect location for the powder room to be placed in the plan of the house.

From the interior, the plan is just as detailed. The stair hall is the place where the applied paneling that begins in the side entrance actually has its fullest expression. First, we pass under the turn of the stair landing in an intimate threshold in the hallway. Then we come into the full height of the space, with one completely paneled wall that is made with a central pair of pilasters that I love so much for their elegant, wide, and here very tall yet low profile; these, too, are taken from the inspiration of that elegant vintage apartment in Rome with the slender paneling, which determined the side entrance. This space is also where I first drew the simple, small, almost quarter-round crown moulding that then went into Dan's office and the kitchen bedroom. The crown sits on the top of those tall pilasters that climb all the way up the height of the hall. It then carries on up the rest of the staircase walls. The whole of this wall is painted in the fresh, stony white strié finish that also continues on from the side entrance.

Turning into the stairs, the two windowed walls of the hall change from paneling to wallpaper. From the beginning, it was a special, first inclination to connect the hall to the gardens all around with a botanical-style paper—and another key moment in the house to create this type of prominent, patterned wall. Considering all

A favorite, delicate, triangular-shaped, painted Italian table holds a bronze Grand Tour classical rabbit, in the corner of the stair landing. Dahlias, Queen Anne's lace, clematis, and hydrangeas reflect the tones of the stair hall.

the surface area of this very tall space, I did feel there had to be a complementary balance between what would be papered and what would be paneled and painted. In a *World of Interiors* story from some time ago, I had seen an absolutely luminous image of a stairwell covered in a beautiful foiled paper, something silvery and leafed; and that became the starting point. With the windows letting in so much dreamlike, west-facing dawn light, I thought the hall could feel silvery and enchanted in a similar way. For all its architecture and height, the space did seem to want something very pretty and soft.

While designing this hall, I decided to hang a collection of small Impressionist paintings all through the stairwell. I began this collection long ago, when I was just starting out myself, with a few tiny American Impressionist landscapes. Over many years the paintings have come together in various types and qualities, with such a range in their subjects, but I never had the chance to assemble them in one place. Set atop the silvered wallpaper, the hall has such a soft, poetic lens on these studies of foliage, gardens, architecture, and even portraits, in the way that the whole house is about gardens and design and art. And from here we move into the library, which is filled with books, art, design, photography, and architecture, where these elements transform into something more.

At the foot of the stairs, the alabaster figure is known as *The Roman Wrestler*, after Canova. I found this mid-nineteenth-century example with a series of other bronze Grand Tour sculptures at an auction in Paris. The light reflects in an Italian gessoed mirror across the stair hall, to an eighteenth-century, shield-shaped Venetian mirror among the paintings. On a George II, marble top Queen Anne–style table, peonies and roses from the height of the garden in June are arranged in another Murano glass vase that I created with Seguso in Venice, for my store. The Charles X bouillotte lamp is the constant light of the stairhall; the Lalique pigeon is always here. The natural form wood tray is from our travels in Japan.

ONE TREE HOUSE

Tucked away on the lower paneled incline of the stairway, I placed this delicate Tina Modotti photograph as an intended pause. With its empty courtyard and single tree, the image, *Fachada del Colegio*, is so peaceful to me, and special as well for being an unusual architectural subject for the photographer. I've always loved the dreamlike beauty of the façade and the particular stillness in the image, among the pictures I've collected by Tina Modotti. When putting the Library together, it felt so much a kindred spirit to this 1920s-style, many-windowed building, with our own large, old sycamore tree, just in front of the house. In my imagination it is the talisman for this tree and this house. Yet, for all its small size and its paleness, in its light frame on the light stairwell, the picture somehow draws one in and invites a longer look. Sometimes the tiniest of gestures can do that more powerfully than big or loud ones. The photograph has magic in it.

I was inclined to pair the picture with a beautifully carved, nineteenth-century Savonarola chair: counter-points of dark and light, bold and diminutive. This is one among many fine pieces that I found in Hudson, New York, at one of my most trusted and favorite antique dealers, Theron Ware. Numerous discoveries, finds, and unique furniture from this store are filtered through the house and are especially to be found in this stair hall.

I've always loved the elegant, folding, slatted x-form of this type of chair. One sees them often in images of 1920s houses, of a time when classical revival styles were very popular. I am always interested in finding and restoring antiques like this for clients' houses as well, for all the layers of history and antiquity they bring along with them, and the particular hand of the century when they were reinterpreted. Neoclassical things spool back in time and carry so much design reverence with them, for all the forms and ideas that have been passed along from generation to generation. In this photograph, this chair, all the surrounding architecture, I want those echoes to be true for the entire feeling of this house.

Fachada del Colegio by Tina Modotti. The title is written in her own hand on the back of the piece; it must have been a very special place. Here I paired it with a mahogany, Italian Renaissance-style Savonarola folding chair. The slanted paneling is a clue to the small powder room hidden here, underneath the stairs.

I'd always imagined tucking a powder room under the stairs as part of the stair hall construction. With an extra odd step down to go inside, this is one of those eccentric, irregular rooms in the house that suggests the fitting of new roles into older spaces. In a particular English spirit, we chose a warm, golden yellow called Dijon for the walls. In the evenings, the room glows in the quiet white hallway. Many of the furnishings and early photographs are from the late nineteenth century—the era between the two parts of the house, where the centuries meet in the stair hall. I especially love the antique penmanship exercise that says, "Cheer up, seek success."

I sometimes explain the "knuckles" and passages in a home as the curious transitions beyond the main rooms that get you from here to there. How they are worked through can make such a difference. All of these unique spaces make up an enormous amount of the design that I love to imagine, detail, and pay attention to. These idiosyncrasies and varied elaborations combine to give the feeling of a real history here, with a series of preserved and reworked spaces that were compiled as the house grew and changed.

This first landing on the stair is one of those particular knuckles. It was necessary to cross the hall at this level in the middle of the stairs in order to access the art balcony over the library room. We enter that hidden passage through what we call the art room, where more works of all periods are stored. The late Renaissance allegorical painting pictured through the doorway is by Alessandro Tiarini. The narrow door to the art room is a whimsical, old-feeling step up over the baseboard; it is concealed by more hanging paintings and a continuation of the hall's wallpaper. On a Biedermeier table, the art deco plaster sculpture of two figures by Lucien Gibert is from the same Parisian auction as *The Roman Wrestler* at the bottom of the stairs.

Of all the many materials and choices in the house, Dan and I spent as much time thinking about the right paper here as on anything we did. We spent long months looking at all kinds of options, from silvered and foiled to more naturalistic and green motifs, to patterns with a chinoiserie element. We looked and looked at so many papers directly in the space, in every kind of light, morning and evening. But the silvery idea lingered. Eventually we discovered this very lovely and mystical GP & J Baker wallpaper called Oriental Bird. It was ivory with a light pink cast, almost oyster colored, and the most delicate of chinoiserie-style silvered branches. On the walls it was wondrous, like a garden in the snow.

With all the windows and the subtle glint of the silver, the whole stair hall glows. I love how the space comes to life just as much in the luster of evening lamplight. It is truly such a light box, bright even in the colder seasons, that it's become one of the places where we bring plants in to winter over—delicate lemon and orange trees included. It's essentially our sunroom in the Library, like the sunroom right across from it at the Academy that is always filled with plants. Now we have these spots in both houses, along with the greenhouse, to look after as much as we can possibly take in from the garden.

The light-filled upstairs landing, looking over to the Academy. The whisper of pink in this paper was a perfect bridge to our favorite pale Tissue Pink paint color in the master bedroom. The Japanese bronze lamp belonged to a friend and most favorite antique dealer, Robert Altman, for many years.

Modern to medieval. A special sculptural Carlo Mollino oak side chair, from Casa del Sole in Cervinia, Italy, sits under a large panel of traditional handmade Turkish "ebru" marbled paper. I think of the Mollino chair as being as pure of form and craft as any of the Greek or Roman objects in the house. These elegant, complex medieval keys came from the London sale of the extraordinary private collection of Roger Warner, a renowned antiquarian and dealer of early English furniture and artifacts. The other treasure from his collection is the red velvet sleeping chair in the library room.

TREE OF LIFE

The details of the main staircase are drawn from elements of my grandparents' stairway in their house in Hamilton, New York, which I knew so well and loved as a little boy. The newel post comes most directly from that house. I reinterpreted the form to make multiple posts in different sizes that punctuate the staircase as it turns and rises up. Then I paired the posts with a more intricately fluted baluster to add grace and age to the whole structure. These pieces of the staircase were hand-milled for the house by a wonderful woodworker we found in New Hampshire, who brought such careful and individual skill to creating all the many parts. With the paneled architecture, the silvery walls, and all the windows, I did feel that this was a place to do something elaborate, something carved and then completely crisp and white.

Against the white staircase in this sunny hall, I knew that the steps would be anchoring in dark walnut-stained wood. This light and dark pairing returns in the staircase down to the studio from the library room—a combination that I always find so clean, tailored, and handsome. In the Library, really all the stairs are purposefully the reverse of the light and dark mix at the Academy, where the stairs and floors are white, and elements of the banisters are black. But for the main stair, in this especially pretty, dreamlike hall, I also wanted to have a runner to complete the richness and warm hush of steps going up to the house's private rooms.

The matter of what to place on the treads was resolved in one of the unexpected finds for the house. I happened to come across several small runners of this beautiful, traditional Tree-of-Life Oushak carpet, designed and made by my friend, Alpaslan Basdogan, of Asia Minor Carpets. I loved the abstracted motif on such a surprisingly graphic, dark chocolate ground. Alp was able to find just the right amount of carpets needed to complete the stairs—everything he had at the time. The essence of the carpet, a tree of life, was such a powerful metaphor for so much that I wanted to create here, with nature branching through the house in so many directions. Now we can't imagine anything else that could be more right or more meaningful as an expression of this library and garden.

The view down the stairs. The lantern is English oak, found in London. It was hanging in the Aero shop for many years and I always loved it—it was one of those things that never sold. I decided to reglaze it with this particularly wavy seeded glass, and paint it in glossy Litchfield Green. It was meant to be for the screen porch, and the Elizabeth chandelier was for this space. And then in the moment, against the pink chinoiserie paper, I took the chandelier down and put this bolder lantern up, loving it here and forever happy that the Elizabeth chandelier is in the kitchen bedroom.

and contemplative, to have this airy white floor.

The opening down the stairs into the studio equally serves to add brightness and intrigue to the library room. The whole structure of the downstairs was lifted up so that there would be deep, open window wells to allow light into the lower level, which would also stream upward through this room. And this, too, lifted the kitchen up from the library floor a few gentle steps, for a different view over the room. Above, from the second floor, I carved out two balconies from the height of the library—one balustraded gallery along the east wall of the room and another balcony that cantilevers over the kitchen. The latter balcony has a gentle, arched opening that follows the tall, vaulted double-height ceiling of the kitchen area. The room flows up and goes down, and is illuminated from both above and below.

The primary library-dining table in the middle of the room is so much like the plan of the Academy living room with its defining, centered long table. Of course, that lofty room wasn't originally a living space, either. It was the 1833 open classroom in a schoolhouse. So, between these two

houses, we have a classroom an room that we live in. We are, i forever students.

THIS PAGE AND OVERLEAF: The library room is reflected in the mirror above the oversize fir The fireplace was inspired by a fascinating Edwin Lutyens design that had a window withir interior wall. The mantel is made of highly figured Calacatta Paonazzo marble for the surr along with a carved and rusticated, seventeenth-century-style Italian gilded frame casing end of the room, the giant eighteenth-century Georgian cabinet sits between doors to the

Into the Library

In every way, this large room is what the Library House is for and about. It is a meaningful set of collections and furniture; it is our living and entertaining space; it is an open, high-ceilinged loft. It is the link to the studio below it and the kitchen just steps above it. As considerable as it is in scale, it is a secret wing that is not obvious from the front of the house. Most of all, it is an active and actual library where we keep the growing repository of books, art, and artifacts that we use, study, and take inspiration from every week. Best of all, it is the magical, rich green room that sits right in the middle of the garden.

The Library Room

There are many different routes through the house, but all of them lead to the library room in the garden. It is a discovery when you finally see it, as the house unfolds from the intimate, nineteenth-century shape of the front rooms and hallways into this one giant open room in the back. In fact, the size of the room was modeled on the two vintage, full-floor, industrial work lofts that my store, Aero, occupied in two different locations over the years, downtown in the Soho gallery district of New York City. The library shares exactly the same open feeling and room dimensions and height, with almost fifteen-foot-tall ceilings. For all its architecture and cabinetry, the layers of color and antiques and furniture, all the art and books, this drawing room-library is really a modern loft at heart. I've always just loved a big room.

I do like to put these blended perceptions of the modern and traditional together into the homes I design. In particular, it's important that this room, and the experiment of the whole house around it, aren't really about the reproduction of an old way of life. They're more about an open way to live and work today, among favorite old things. And it is easy to be in this space among them. We use the books all the time. Lately both of us have taken to working at the dining table, shifting back and forth from the kitchen, taking a pause to relax while we prepare dinner or lunch. While the Academy is our home and touchstone, we move over here during the day to work, and to host clients

and business partners: this libr
the energy of all the things in
lected from so many different
It's the place to try out ideas a
by books, antiquities, art, furni
from it all for every part of my
making lighting, dishes, furnit
stores, or homes.

When I began designing
the first that I needed that on
all the parts of my design life
dispersed. This was always wh
door to the Academy was abo
multiplied, as the library room
formal living space and I adde
studio. A major decision was t
related spaces via a large, purp
turning staircase with elegant
of the library room, to take yo
this scale, the opening of the s
up the oversize library into di
more intimate to spend time i

This was also the one room
always wanted to return to the
floors that I have in our apartm
and my offices at Aero, and ne:
love the silhouettes of all the m
against it. The paleness makes
and it's especially nice in this r

PREVIOUS PAGES: Volumes of books fill two tall bookcase bays between the fireplace and t
end of the library room—photography to the left, cookbooks to the right, closer to the kitc
center library-dining table hosts an ever-changing rotation of objects as they come into th
A most extraordinary Christmas gift from Dan is the original 1788 edition of Sir John Soan
Elevations, and Sections of Buildings—a treasure for the library.

F ramed by the railing to the staircase, the primary seating group is anchored by a graphic, diamond-patterned Persian Bakhtiyari rug from the 1850s, and a deep, comfortable, but formally made wing-style sofa. The upholstery is the special and classic note here, a French cut velvet in a very traditional pattern of lions, called Lyon. We chose it in a warm, pale, mustardy yellow that shimmers in the room; this is one of the recurring colors throughout the house. The ottoman is upholstered with a natural madder-dyed Anatolian carpet. There are two diminutive, vintage French club chairs that I'd saved for twenty years—even the upholsterer was amazed that they had never been re-covered. In fact, we found a two-franc coin from 1948 in the old upholstery. Another low, vintage, bleached oak bergère is covered in a rich, gilded, and grey-blue floral velvet; the colorway is evocatively named Black Pearl. This created an even more complex mix of patterns with the carpet.

Luxuriant, colorful, patterned fabrics have prominence in this house, in a fashion that is admittedly different from the pale and subtler neutrals I often use. This upholstery allowed me to create something dressier and with the richer personality I wanted at the Library. For all its elegance, we actually use our furniture here in a completely relaxed, easy way. This is always something I think about, in how to use traditional and luxurious elements and make them useful now, modern and not just of the past.

The main library room carpet is one of the more rare things in the house. For some reason, the pattern and color always make me think of an old Errol Flynn movie. The Bakhtiyari people were pastoral nomads and their name is best translated as "companion of chance" or "bearer of good luck." The natural dyes for this carpet include saffron, which would have been enormously precious and rare at that time. Additionally, the deep green color in the carpet is so unique that even modern testing cannot determine what created it. In particular, I love the scrolled motif set within each large diamond.

This is a working library of design of all kinds. The books are divided into different sections: photography, art, architecture. There is a very large section on interiors and decorative arts. We have a full section on gardens, and then one on regions and cultures—New England and Long Island, but also England, France, Japan, all places we are intrigued by. And then there is an extensive collection of cookbooks, old and new. Hanging on the photography bookcase is one of the most special pieces of art, *Saint Jerome in His Study*, Albrecht Dürer, 1514. This important pre-Renaissance engraving is one of a group of three defining allegories. Symbolically collected for this Library, Saint Jerome represents theological and contemplative life.

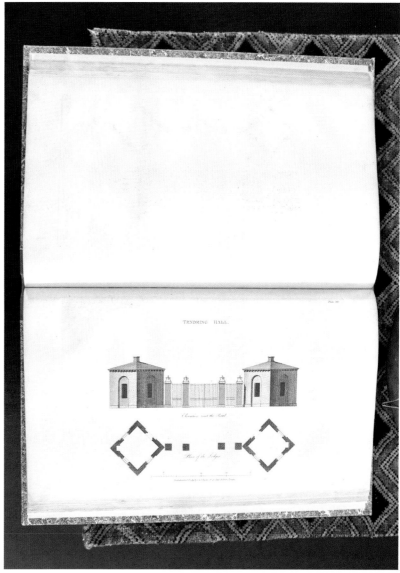

Dividing the living area from the kitchen is my own Leland drop-leaf dining table, which I designed as a desk, a library table, and a dining table. The profile borrows from a Danish Modern 1950s design, though it also echoes the drop-leaf tables that were popular in the 1830s and '40s. Dishes and serving pieces fill the cabinet to the left; the bar is to the right. The table is surrounded by a set of Duncan Phyfe Federal mahogany chairs with remarkably beautiful paw feet and perfect slender lines. These chairs were originally made in the 1820s as a wedding present for a New York family, and they remained in the same family until the 1960s. They were worn and bruised and showed their two hundred years of age by the time I saw them, but I was just so charmed that they were made and had existed for their whole life in New York City. After restoring the chairs, I covered the seats in my Matthew striped velvet, in a color called Claret, that feels both traditional and modern. The John Soane book rests open on the table.

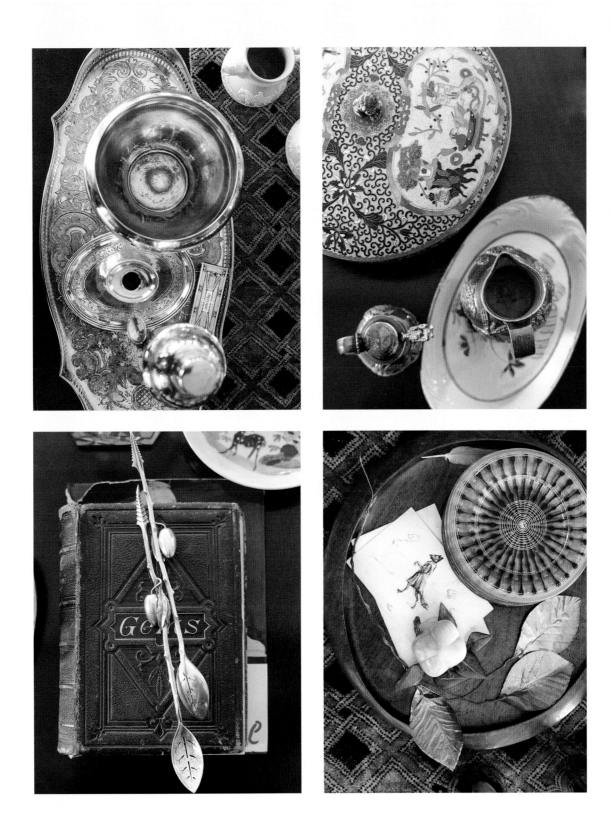

Resting place. Having a library-center table is a key idea for me. I will often use a long dining table as a desk-studio-library space that can be filled and layered with books and objects. Just like the long table in the conference room at our studio office in the city, our table here in this library is most often the first place where new and collected things settle when they come into the house. They do a turn on the table as we live with them before deciding on where they will eventually go.

Ancient and modern, across the room. A Hellenistic Greek terra-cotta head of a god or athlete was once part of a standing figure of impressive proportions. I created the pedestal for it to emulate the life-size height of the imagined figure. It watches over the library room from a Kaare Klint, circa 1930 sideboard, nested beneath the proscenium casing of the kitchen. From this vantage point, the main stairs are visible across the threshold into the stair hall. On the far side of the room, in the Georgian cabinet, a Picasso faience vessel from Madoura looks back among the books.

I've always been intrigued by the grand conservatory and drawing room spaces in old English country houses, which are divided into smaller rooms-within-a-great-room that fit together. For this room I used a low screen and a series of wonderful carpets to make different areas around the fireplace and in front of the staircase, each of which was then centered on its own group of furniture.

Because this house is an invention rather than a restoration, there are many interlocking inspirations in the architectural makeup of the room. All of the cabinetry details on the bookcases come from the lines and profiles of the Georgian cabinet at the end of the room. Those profiles worked with the larger Wren mouldings that came into this space from the front of the house. I designed the recessed, paneled ceiling using a very particular moulding that returns inward, to create the beautiful shadow line that makes the paneling stand out against the ceiling plane: this helps to make the scale of the room feel both older and more measured. These features all have so much to do with how the building feels tailored and potentially from another time. It really would have been a completely different house without their intricacy and surface character.

A view down the length of the room, with the long balcony overhanging the portico entrance. A pair of my Farlane chandeliers, specially made in silver plate, hangs on either end of the room, from low profiled beams on the paneled ceiling. We found the very large, Renaissance-style, early twentieth-century celestial library globe at Christie's, and of course thought of this wonderful, big library room to put it in.

AT THE CENTER OF THE ROOM

With such a large room to plan, I always had in mind key antiques and pieces of furniture that were crucial to how the library was to be formed and how it could feel more personal. Central among these, both in the room and in our searchings, was the tremendously special, 1760s Georgian serpentine-front desk that I knew would go right between the fireplace and the living space, and make up the axis between the long library table and the studio stairs. In its way, the desk is the miniature of the huge Georgian cabinet in the room, both made in the same decade, both so exceptionally handsome and magical to me.

The desk came from the wonderful auction of the Tom Devenish collection, about ten years ago. Mr. Devenish was a dealer in fine English and especially eighteenth-century furniture who had a legendary store on Madison Avenue for nearly fifty years. His was one among a small set of the most important stores of period furnishings, including Stair & Company and Florian Papp, that I frequented and certainly learned from when I started my career, working for Ralph Lauren. Where the other stores had things that were perhaps a bit more polished and Continental, I was always struck by the beautiful age and original patina, flawlessly of the period, of the furniture in Mr. Devenish's store. Its crowded, smoky rooms intrigued me as an older, singular, and mysterious kind of place, maybe more like the shops in London, for all the finery more like a classic antique store. As a proprietor, Mr. Devenish was known to be a bit of a tough character, but he loved and knew everything about every piece in his care. I had the chance to meet him in his shop and never forgot it. To have one of his pieces in this room is really as much about my history, my practical education as I was becoming a designer, as it is about loving unique and remarkable things.

Seated with the George II desk from Mr. Devenish are two of a set of four Danish Jugendstil mahogany neoclassical armchairs. Jugendstil was the northern European equivalent of the French art nouveau movement in the late nineteenth and very early twentieth centuries, known for its affinity for natural forms and structures and its emphasis on absolute craft. The special art deco desk lamp is in green Bakelite and turned birchwood. I kept it for many years at Aero, waiting for the right spot, until I put it on this Georgian desk—a central and perfect place in the middle of this room.

Tucked in by the fireplace is a most important George II sleeping chair, dating to 1755. I gently restored the frame and re-covered it in a red velvet very similar to the color of the original upholstery, and I designed the companion ottoman. It's as comfortable today as it was centuries ago, and centuries ago, it was as novel as it feels today. I have always loved its low lines and startling modernism for a chair that is over two hundred fifty years old.

There is a low, upholstered, green box-pleated silk screen that shelters the seating area around the fireplace. The Georgian desk is to one side and on the other is the antique bone leather sofa from my 57th Street apartment of years ago, with a Georgian gateleg table. This is where I will most often go to pause and read in the house. For the north end of the room, I made floor-to-ceiling cabinets that are integrated on either side of the kitchen entrance, to hold various collections of china, silver, and barware. This full wall is green—the only place in the room where the cabinetry is green on the exterior, paired with the reddish-brown interiors of the cabinets.

Library Color. When I'm designing libraries and cabinets of all kinds, a favorite detail is to give the interior niches and shelves a contrasting or deeper color that can be glimpsed through the books and objects. In the past I've used dark eggplant and tones of leather; here, we chose a deep, red, bordeaux-like brown.

Graphic light and dark anemones are an ever-favorite flower; a hand-painted Italian tureen has all the blue, leafy green, and red of the room; the pale, feathery blue of Japanese delphinium is lovely in this vase we made years ago for Aero, that I always have flowers in for this room. The china cabinet holds part of my collection of hand-painted and transfer-ware dishes and serving pieces.

Antique collections of silver, crystal, and American and Irish cut and pressed stemware in the bar shimmer inside the green and red cabinet. The petite nineteenth-century French writing desk is made with ormolu mounts and contrasting kingwood and tulipwood, adding another elegance to the American elements of the room. I chose it specifically, elaborate as it is, to be the small bar in the library. A very beautiful Georgian silver toddy ladle sits on a set of antique marbleized end papers.

In the early plans for the library, we strongly considered painting this room yellow. I've forever loved all the wonderful large yellow drawing rooms and conservatory rooms in English country houses; yet we were pulled to something richer here. Understanding from the Academy how the beautiful bright southern light travels across the garden where this room sits, I knew we could lean into a hushed, deeper color. This room called to be green. After much experimenting we settled on a dark ivy green for the walls called Southern Vine, and the reddish brown for the interior of the cases, called Townsend Harbor Brown. To make the room brighter and enunciate all the millwork, the cabinetry and casings for the bookshelves were then painted in a fawnlike, almost butterscotch, pale beige with a strié finish, still an heirloom combination with such a warm patina, as you would see in those yellow English drawing rooms. And then the room has its modern, loft-white floors to lighten things even more.

In the corner is a 1928 Steinway piano that arrived on Christmas years ago as a gift from me to Dan. It occuples the back of the gallery behind the staircase and fills the warm acoustics of this vaulted room with music when he plays. Above, the ebonized, classical scrolled bench, at the garden door behind the piano, is by Paul Frankl.

Coming in from the allée, the wide portico entrance is situated beneath the long catwalk balcony that we reach from the upstairs landing. The screen porch and my office are to either side of the bookcases. This particular set of cases holds a section about special places and regional subjects, including books both vintage and new about France, Japan, Italy, and Ireland, and others on important designers. I love the old handsome parchment books with glided columns on the spines, behind the 1904 Edward Curtis photograph of an Indian chief, *Haschezhini-Navaho*. On the table, I've always been taken with this small bronze of a man sowing seeds, an optimistic figure about prosperity and of course connected to my sense of the garden.

At the End
of the Room

When I was drawing up the earliest plans of the house, I happened upon this enormous, very beautiful Georgian breakfront cabinet at Christie's. There it was at the end of a long gallery, a piece so large that it was almost homeless in terms of where it could possibly go; it was too big for anyone to use. At that point I was pretty certain of what the height of the library room was going to be, and so I was quickly able to determine that this cabinet would, miraculously, fit. In every way I built the room around it.

This cabinet is truly a magnificent handmade piece, dating from the late 1760s. I love the way it was put together with such ordered, easy grace in its many classical parts, so elegant but with imperfections, too. The paneled doors with their high, elongated, geometric fretwork panes are so charming. The large pediment and mouldings have such wonderful proportion and tailored, intact detail. Yet for all its remarkable handcraft and just the pure fineness and patina of the mahogany it was made of two hundred and fifty years ago, I was able to buy this piece for far less than it would take to make it today—even to just buy the wood. There certainly needed to be something this stunning to hold attention at the end of the room.

The cabinet stands nearly fifteen feet high. I designed the dimensions of the room around it. It sits on a gallery behind the railing of the stairs to the studio, with relatively little floor space in front of it. There's something so nice about that to me, the surprising intimacy of stepping up close to this huge piece of furniture that from a distance makes up an entire wall of the room. A last detail that Dan and I added was the pair of tall, white painted neoclassical lamps, found in London.

Treasures of many eras come together behind the fretwork doors of the Georgian cabinet. A wonderful piece is the Steuben Gazelle Bowl, designed by Sidney Waugh in 1935. Elegant art deco gazelles run around the bowl in a style reminiscent of Greek friezes and terra-cottas. It is the balance of colored glass, etched glass, and dark and light silhouettes here that appeals to me.

More profiles and colors: Steuben glass, rock crystal, Georgian Nailsea glass, an ancient spear, opalescent, golden Murano glass, a beautiful cobalt blue Georgian glass decanter, a spiral-cut Indian glass candlestick, Greek terra-cotta. To the glass I added the shadowy silhouettes of a fine bronze Buddha and an American nineteenth-century felted beaver fur top hat.

Once I had the cabinet, I planned its surroundings from the beginning. As I was working on the design of the room overall, I had in mind the Beauport House in Gloucester, Massachusetts, which I'd always admired. Similar to great American estates like Winterthur, with collections of American decorative arts, Beauport is a rambling turn-of-the-century summer "cottage" built by the collector Henry Davis Sleeper, to display his many holdings of fine and folk art, architectural artifacts, and especially glass of all kinds.

Of the many wonderful details and rooms at Beauport, one idea in particular stuck with me. Sleeper had built shelves directly in front of a large window in his central hall and filled them with a collection of amber glass bottles, chalices, and candlesticks. Enclosed in this alcove behind a screen of finely paneled lead glass, the glass collection is famously backlit and sculptural, with a beautiful, soft glow from the light filtering in through the window. Elsewhere, there are more collections of colorful glass—bottle green, amethyst—that are backlit in smaller cabinets and windows.

I wanted to do something like that here, so I sized the window that looks onto the sunken garden to the middle top bay of the cabinet. I removed the wooden back panels and had them refitted with opaque, antiqued glass. With the two high, paned glass doors to the garden and the central window in this cabinet, natural light pours in, giving the whole library its warm radiance—much like the afternoon light I knew so well from the Academy.

Like other places in the house, the Georgian cabinet is a contained library. The collection here is a mix of colorful glass, design and history books, and very special antique books, together with many other objects

that I had long been gathering up for this room. The cabinet holds some pieces of elegant, classical etched Steuben crystal, along with smoky and various blue and purple, nineteenth-century Baltimore, English, and Nailsea glass; yellow Vaseline glass; and pieces of Murano glass. There are also shapely Georgian pitchers and vessels of exquisitely detailed, low-relief sprigware that I have been collecting more recently. At the end of the view through the whole house, these objects are celebrated as they were absolutely meant to be.

The Steuben covered glass jar titled "The Sciences" is part of a set of four jars also including "The Arts," "Industry," and "Agriculture." Next to the glass is a set of three, quite perfect, black-glazed classical Greek gutti—terra-cotta oil lamps—from the third century BC.

OVERLEAF: The cabinet holds a group of Picasso Madoura pitchers in among the old things and books. The largest grey pitcher with portrait faces dates to 1954. There's a mix of beautiful old novels with more reference books, including my own two design books.

A ROOM WITH A VIEW

For us, living and working in New York City makes this retreat at the Library feel all the more like we are in the faraway peace of the country. It's an enchantment that comes when we leave the city and shed the pace and stress of the week—that impulse to head toward nature, whether the beach, the river, the mountains, the woods, or the countryside, and slow down.

Our new country house would not be what it is if we did not have these special gardens all around, with such connections between indoors and outdoors. From the doors at the end of the library room, we can see all the way through our walled garden to the wilder woodland end of this property, and feel as though we have a view into another time, or even another place: the South, or England, or France. In fine weather the tall doors stay open and we easily step back and forth between worlds.

I've never thought that different worlds simply have to collide. To me, they can be great soul mates. City and country, home and studio, memory and now, coexist in this house. There are echoes of New York in the essential structure of the doors and windows that guide us outside from this room. For example, the tall scale and large panes of all the window panels in this section of the house are based off the overall window size and individual panes of a favorite old building on MacDougal Street in Greenwich Village that belongs to the New York University School of Law.

When I was new to New York and in school at the Cooper Union, I always looked around at all the buildings I admired as I walked in the Village and Union Square. I was making a mental catalog of the specific shapes and proportions that I liked, which I imagined that I might use someday. I still do this today, wherever I go. For this library wing, it felt just right that these tall windows were from an academic building rather than a house or residential building. It also made sense to me, in a kind of shared downtown language, that this Greenwich Village building would be from the same, older Manhattan heritage as my Aero lofts in Soho. As we look through windows here borrowed from that past, into gardens that were planted so that we could have a more restful and grounded present, it feels again as though the world awaits us.

Alignment occurs throughout the house as a means of extending sight lines and views; it also creates intuitive order among the varied parts of the architecture. The tall door on the east side of the Georgian cabinet aligns with the stone doorway in the brick wall that takes us into the walled garden, and all the way through to the far end of the property. On the other side of the cabinet, another tall door is aligned with a moon window in the brick wall that also looks into the garden.

The Screen Porch

There are three openings under the catwalk balcony that spans the east side of the library room. There is the portico entrance, which is the main threshold into the library. On its far side, tucked into its leafy corner of the house and the garden, is my office. And on the closer side of the portico is our airy and essential screen porch.

At the Academy, the screen porch off of our kitchen has always been the favorite and all-important place for entertaining. Having a similar screen porch here was a must for entertaining in the same way. In the configuration of this section of the white brick wing of the house, an open-air screen porch was the natural match for my office on the other side of the portico and for the portico itself. Where the porch is open to the garden, this new and special columned entrance to the library is open to the sky above.

Because of the structure of this part of the building, the height I could give to the screen porch was a wonderful opportunity. The windows from the high main stair hall set the proportion of this space on one side. And then the porch aligns with a view of the allée where I'd added a new small garden unto itself, in front of a handsome little garden shed. In its relationship to this separate garden, the porch does feel somewhat hidden and intimate. It is such a nice place, where the garden really does come into the house, especially in the summer when we are in here so much, with the doors and the windows wide open. This is the spot we gravitate to for dinner and often even for lunch—an open-air jewel box of a space that is as important in its own way as the lush and formal library that it opens onto.

Between those surroundings, inside and outside, I wanted the porch to have its own time-twisting personality. Two of its walls are made of the outer white brick of the building, and its bluestone flooring is echoed in the lower garden steps. But those exterior materials are handled like part of an interior. The floors are laid in a unique running bond like some of the dark marble floors inside the house.

The porch has its own singular mullions and millwork details: there is an inner balustrade that runs on the two outside-facing walls, with handsome working shutters and full-wall screens that are removable from the windows. For porches and open-air spaces, I always like these elements to be functional and real, but also nicely finished. I love the way all the wood is crafted, and the fine hook-and-eye hardware that holds the screens in. I love that the porch reveals the surprise of the staircase, how they look one into the other, equally as light and airy outside as the hall is inside. You can't quite tell which came first, the interior or this lovely space beside it, and that mystery adds to the free spirit of the house.

Dappled light pours into the screen porch on a summer day. It is positioned across from the shingled Academy garage, with a gentle view of the walkway through my little flower garden. This is the open-air room in the Library where we very often entertain and have dinner.

FOUND OBJECTS

There is a certain chemistry that can happen between pieces for a room or even a table setting. Sometimes elements from such different worlds and eras find each other and are meant to be together. It's intuitive. Things just fall into sync and they create pleasure in their combination, though one couldn't really explain why exactly they feel so pleasing.

That's what occurred with this fish slice and platter. More than a still life image, these are real partners that are always paired for serving. The fish slice is Georgian, and as with many Georgian things, it has such an elegant simplicity that can feel almost modern. I loved the soft wear on the green bone handle, the sculpture of it, the laurel etching on the silver. Near about the same time that I bought this antique, I also found the Swedish midcentury oval platter. With that piece, it was all about the fine shape of the rounded oval, the simple raised border, the size—such a beautiful form. The mossy green glaze is a color of the period, but in the context of the slice, it somehow felt English and much older, too. And there it was—Georgian and Swedish midcentury modern. Two things that wouldn't have met in their own times, but which make each other better and more wonderful together.

This is much the idea behind many of the things I like to pair—the modern in the antique and the antique in the modern. And it's an especially nice and creative way to collect and combine tableware. Both Dan and I believe in using all of our collections on a regular basis, to enjoy them as part of everyday life. And it's our routine to stop and set a beautiful table.

On any given day we might grill fish in the wood-fired oven in the garden house and bring it back here to the screen porch for dining. We'll use the Swedish platter and the English slice, but also my favorite Italian hand-painted dinner plates, batik napkins from India, bamboo flatware from France. Some is old; some is new. It's a collection of goods that we find special, that have found their way here, from the many places and traditions we are interested in.

A real collection of tableware that we use—in the colors of the garden and a combination of favorite pieces—awaits an afternoon on the screen porch.

Around the table and toward the stair hall. The furnishings in the screen porch are easy and simple, as much of the garden as they are of the house. I found the French Victorian mahogany oval table in Southampton and loved it for its worn and cracked grey marble top. Amethyst goblets from my early home collection with Marshall Field's feel right with this colorful table setting. The bench filled with candlewick and ticking stripe pillows was a Gothic church pew that had been on someone's porch in upstate New York. I painted the bench and table my favorite Litchfield Green, the same color as the shutters on the house.

Under the windows to the stair hall I placed a Gothic serving table with a white marble top, which was also discovered out on Long Island. The group of three old bonsai here is so special. I found them recently and made a safe home for them during the summer in the screen porch; they overwinter in the Academy.

My Office

In the farthest corner of the house, under the shade of the copper beech tree, and in the center of all the gardens, sits my office. I chose this spot amid the gardens just as Dan chose the front room full of light for his office. They are bookends to each other in many ways, and both very Continental rooms at heart, at the two edges of the house.

This is a small room, but it has one paired and two single large, tall windows that extend all the way to the floor. As my office actually exists in the space of the library, the windows are matched to the two tall, double-hung windows on the fireplace wall. It's a subtle millwork detail, but for these three windows, different from the library windows, I chose to picture frame the window casings all the way around them, much like the large double bay window at the top of the main stairs. When it works rather than having a sill, this is a favorite window casing treatment. Additionally, the house that my grandmother grew up in, on Pleasant Street in Hamilton, New York, had windows that went down to the floor; it was a design detail I'd always remembered and had long wanted to use in a special way in my own house someday. I'm enchanted by these windows, on all three sides of the room.

The idea here from the start was to have fully upholstered walls. This is one of the places in the house where I was inclined to have more richness of pattern, and like the stair hall, I wanted to have a botanical design. I chose the classic Nympheus block-print fabric from Lee Jofa, an all-time favorite that

I've used many times in different projects. The original was made in a very water-garden-like color palette, and it had existed in just this one color for as long as I knew it. A number of years back, I was invited to recolor the pattern. I chose to create two deeper, darker colorways in palettes I like very much—a very deep, rich blue called Teal and an amethyst-colored eggplant called Aubergine; this is the one that I chose

A light khaki-colored and gilded Wedgwood inkwell sits on my desk among books and objects. It's been with me and on one or another of my desks for years.

for my office. I've always used this fabric on its reverse side, whether on furniture or walls; the block-printed color bleeds through in such a soft way that gives the gentle impression of a watercolor painting on linen. Nested among the gardens, with so much window light and this floral flowing across the walls, the office is like a magical, Impressionist conservatory.

From the ebonized black of my Italian bureau plat desk to the more than twenty shades of deep, colorful color on the walls, the room has a very intended richness. I was interested in creating a contrast with the natural lightness of the space, including a pale carpet and the luster of pastel yellow-striped silk drapes. And with one of the few crystal chandeliers in the house, there is something so dreamy and lovely, always shimmering and light, daytime and nighttime, in here. On the edge of light and dark, I'm reminded of how the first interior of my 57th Street apartment was also like this, ivory and deep walnut, soft and rich at the same time, and about the way that dark silhouettes are so intriguing in a light space. Even though that was, at the time, my new city apartment, and it was more modern in style, this room reminds me of those earlier days. Now, the office is more layered and more refined, and the silhouettes of the tall windows and the furniture stand out against a colorful background.

In the early evenings, something about this room calls us. This is where we settle in with the dogs for a pause or a drink with friends before dinner; it's their favorite place to be as the sun drifts into the magic hour and the little room shines, with all the flowers and trees around, both inside and outside.

My office as seen from the library. This is a sitting room that is part of the library in many ways, where I come to think and sit in the sunlight amid the gardens. And like both my office at the Academy and Dan's office here, it is a room full of small and meaningful design souvenirs and most loved furniture.

Windows on all sides. The office sits in the southeast corner of the house. The windowed wall behind the sofa looks onto the open portico entrance. Facing the sunken garden, my desk is the treasure of the room, a wonderful, ebonized, Italian 1940s *bureau plat*. Dan and I saw it in London in the window of Colefax and Fowler, when it was on Brook Street near Claridge's hotel, before the company moved out of that beloved location. Even on my first trips to London, it was such a treat to go that fabled, rambling brick town house. I admired the desk and we moved along, but on Christmas Eve that year, truckers appeared at the Academy and there it was, a surprise gift from Dan.

Against the Nympheus pattern on the walls and in the corners of the room. A special, rare sailor's word book is both humorous and fascinating to read. I use it for naming and it is something I found in particular for the Academy years ago. Behind it, a spiral glass bowl from very early Aero days. The tall, gilded iron, midcentury chinoiserie lamp is one of a pair. Above: a romantic hand-colored nautical print by John Taylor Arms, circa 1920. An American Impressionist nocturne landscape from the late nineteenth century. Garden flowers in a heavy, Irish cut-crystal urn; one sits on my desk, the other sits on the dining table in the library room. A fine, beautifully detailed, early nineteenth-century nocturne painting. A Roman Imperial marble torso of a satyr, from the second century AD.

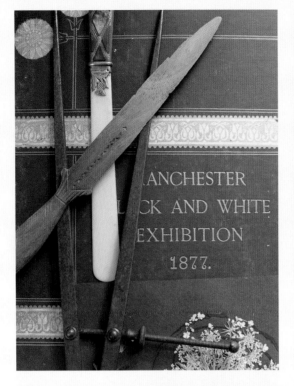

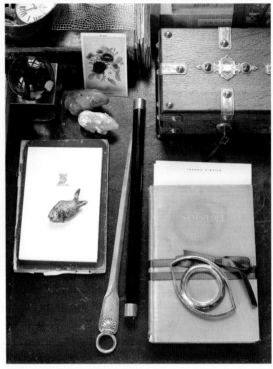

Collections on the desk and deskside. I found my traditional and classical, late eighteenth-century Directoire bergère and fauteuil at auction, glossy and covered in silk. They appealed to me for this office—the larger bergère at my desk and this smaller one set to the side. I kept them brightly polished and changed the upholstery to lambskin leather with a spaced nailhead trim. The fauteuil is always stacked with beautiful books that I am working with and ones that have been special gifts. On my desk: A primitive letter opener I've always had, together with another one from Dan's and my trip to Ireland. An Hermès eye magnifier from Dan. The vintage rotary phone is one of three in the house that ring over from the Academy. The others are in the kitchen and the laundry room.

I love this view from the office looking back into the library. Many times the placement of a doorway is so much about the view it frames outside the room, and that was so purposefully the case here. This tall door aligns all the way across the library to the window behind Dan's piano. The eighteenth-century French Régence bergère is one of a truly beautiful pair that came with much earlier leopard skin upholstery intact from the 1950s. We restored the chairs and left the upholstery as it was. They seemed to belong so completely to this patterned and salonlike space. The Renaissance-style gilded and tooled leather mirror is Italian.

To the Kitchen and Down the Back Stairway

Up a few steps from the library room is our kitchen. As lushly green and wooded as the library with its special, mossy Irish Connemara marble, it's open to the whole room at the literal and emotional center of the house, the place where we cook and recharge. But like much of this house, the kitchen was also designed to be formal and rich, accommodating ideas of entertaining both traditional and modern. This space is the hub that connects us to other housekeeping passages: we pass through a cook's hallway and down a back stairway to rooms for laundry, wine, and other pantries.

The Kitchen

I love to design kitchens. I especially like to make kitchens that people will actually use and cook in, that aren't just for show; that feel like real rooms you'd wish to spend time in. I've always thought about the many ways that cooking and dining become the heart of a home for people, and for here, how to bring those warm realities into the modern, outfitted cook's kitchen that we so needed.

All of these considerations factored in to the kind of kitchen, and by extension, other classic and fine house pantry and service spaces, that I could dream of building here. In a sense, I was getting to make my own dream kitchen, with enough rooms to envision all the resources and storage I would want or could imagine my clients needing. And we do in fact do most of our cooking here now.

For practicality, I was inspired by the traditional sequestering of work areas that occurs in Old World kitchens, made up by various cooking rooms. To have the best from both worlds, I decided from the beginning to create side rooms on either end of the kitchen island, one for the stove, that we call the cooking room, the other for the refrigerator and extra ovens, that we call the pantry. In view from the library room, both of these rooms are relatively hidden by elegant, tall pocketing doors with paneled transoms above, so what is seen of the kitchen is a much more interior-style space without appliances—in the foreground, the railing around the breakfast table; in the center, the bold, large, walnut island, with details of an early English great hall table and a dark green marble top that is panelized like an antique console table.

At the back of the kitchen, the central marble sink has a large inset mirror above it that reflects the length of this library room and its light. It is surrounded by picturesque, green Connemara marble that feels like a landscape in its striations and dappled shading. The big surprise in designing this kitchen was the discovery of this magical marble. I came across it on one chance trip to the stoneyard; I'd never seen anything like it before. Being Irish, I was charmed that the marble came from Connemara on the west coast of Ireland: it is more commonly used for small wares and trinkets than for architecture. There were only about eight slabs and I took them all.

Those first slabs made up the high wainscoting and the central marble sink at the back wall. But, we needed more marble to finish the kitchen. From County Galway in Ireland, we looked at photographs of huge, uncut slabs of the marble. We made a best bet, which in itself was an adventure of risk, and had the thick countertops and remaining needed pieces cut. Those pieces were so beautiful, they were set behind the stove and also became the floor of the cooking room and pantry.

PREVIOUS PAGES: A mirror at the center of the Connemara marble wall in the kitchen reflects light from one end of the library room to the other. The open shelves are a favorite detail and a carryover from the carved marble shelves at the Academy. Copper and enamel cookware hang on vintage-style pegboard in the kitchen's back stairway.

Tall pocket doors define the kitchen spaces and close off this room and the pantry room as needed. Above the cooking room is a romantic, French Impressionist, Barbizon School landscape painting.

The kitchen projects into the library with a proscenium-style casing and a balustraded dining area. I placed a gateleg, oval Georgian table and a settee in this landing that we think of as our breakfast room, with a set of wonderful, torqued and twisted, nineteenth-century English pub chairs—each seat individually worn and shaped from use, and so comfortable. This is where we most often eat and entertain. I designed the island based on profiles out of an antique book of early English furniture drawings. I used the faceted border and panelized top of a Georgian console table for the plan of the Verde Vermont marble top. We brought the deco-style handles for the drawers back from Paris. My Gallia stools add lightness to the darker walnut island. Above, a balcony on the upstairs landing overlooks the library. It rises to the top of the second story to give the kitchen its vaulted, airy, elaborate, and arched height.

For the top of the kitchen island I had in mind this black-green Verde Vermont marble to pair with the Connemara marble. It is very unique in color, in particular this stone. There were three odd pieces, remainders really, that I'd looked at for years in a stoneyard, always asking if there was more and always trying to imagine something special to use those pieces for. This kitchen island became the home for that stone.

Tremendously unique like the stone, I love the pure shape of these Georgian silver marrow spoons, especially the five very uncommon marrow serving spoons dating from the 1750s. They were meticulously gathered over decades by a collector who is an absolute expert in Georgian silver and pottery. I have learned so much from him as we've worked together for some years now, choosing the most beautiful silver as well as sprigware ceramics from his collection to add to ours. Between the island and the sink, the kitchen door opens onto the back stairway.

A vintage trestle-base settee found in Southern California sits at the drop-leaf breakfast table, along with the pub chairs. We upholstered it in a charming owl-patterned fabric. The table is so perfectly shaped and sized; I've used it as a template for other client breakfast and garden tables. Between the cooking room and the back stairway, the 1904 oak wall phone is one of the few antique ones in the house that rings here from the Academy. Above it is a 1989 photograph by Richard Misrach, *White Man Contemplating Pyramids*. Small souvenirs amid a collection of candlesticks: a matchbook from Le Voltaire, a favorite restaurant in Paris; a dish I've had since my very first small apartment in New York; an alphabet-pattern notebook from my first home collection for Target.

La Goulue

The Back Stairway

The kitchen leads to the multistory back staircase, which takes us downstairs to the laundry room and various other small rooms and cabinets. I have always liked old houses with a warren of rooms in lovely old basements. There is a particular charm in all the vintage evocations of a back staircase—the second, family stair off of the kitchen that many big and older homes contain. One of the most delicate and important renovations at the Academy, for example, was the reworking of the back staircase from the upstairs to the kitchen, and then to the mudroom and basement. I am forever up and down those stairs and enjoying the lively, winding way of it all.

With the tiered levels of the basement on this side of the studio, this is the point where the house is actually four stories up and down. The staircase starts in the hallway that annexes the kitchen. In one of the tricks of the house, it seems as if it were added later with windows on two sides that give the first landing the feeling of a mudroom from some previous period of the house. First, the window on the left side of the cooking room faces the outside, but the right side looks into the stairwell; the horizontal window on the far right of the staircase lets light into the bathroom of the kitchen bedroom—as if the stair were filled in somehow later or had been enclosed. So we have this continuing mystery of what was built first and what was renovated or reworked later in this traditional utility passage in the house.

The hallway stores a portion of our cookware, with a huge, old, bold pot rack from a hotel in the Adirondacks for our copper pot collection. In a nostalgic nod, I fitted pegboard to the walls, like Julia Child's famous kitchen, and something I had in my first two apartments in New York. Pegboard remains such a practical, chic, inexpensive solution for hanging pans and cooking gear. I've always loved it. I painted it and other cabinetry along the stairway in a shade of sagey green that reminded me of the back pantry hall in my grandmother's house.

I based the railing of the back staircase on a stairway from the Hotel Danieli in Venice. Dan and I had been in Venice, and in this hotel there was a staircase up to our room from the 1940s, in the midst of this older, fantastic, palatial building. I loved its midcentury character and paired balusters. I adapted the design for this space, including how the handrail becomes the newel post as it turns down to the floor.

With its multiple landings, the stairway has something of a country-house feeling in its movement. The first stop off as we go down is a potting sink and the laundry room; and beyond that, a lower level still with the wine room, root cellar, and a cleaning closet. Cabinetry along the way and another set of steps lead to a room of vintage cookware of all kinds and a room of china and glassware. Other passages lead to the studio. All of this is another library in the house, of all kinds of domestic things.

In the back stairway we store and organize copper pots and special cookware. The soft green paint that I used on the pegboard is called Iced Marble. My Pelham Oval sconce and Clark ceiling light are both a certain kind of vintage, graphic, simple shape that I am inclined to design. The painted English cabinet dates to 1910 and holds a tableau of modern vintage artwork and truly one-of-a-kind domestic tableware prototypes.

The Laundry Room

The first main room as we head down the back stairs is the laundry. In terms of floor planning and structuring the house, this was always practically intended to be the space directly below the kitchen, tucked in and fully fitted out in cabinetry and drying racks: I didn't want laundry to be an afterthought. This room is part of the reason that the kitchen is lifted up those few stairs from the kitchen bedroom on one side, and before the building steps down to the library and the studio on the lower level.

Framed and furniture-like closets and cupboards give the room its fitted character. I designed all the special recessed paneled cabinetry around a deep farmhouse sink that also doubles as the place for dog washing and linens that need hand washing. In this vintage spirit, I added beautiful brass latches and hardware that Dan and I found in Paris. The cabinets are finished in the warm, buttery color of aged cream paint.

Anyone who knows me well knows that I actually enjoy doing laundry. There is something quite peaceful about it for me, in the order that comes of it. This laundry room is actually one of my favorite spaces. It is literally the place in the midst of all the designing and doing every week where I slow down. I always wanted to make this a welcoming space in the center of things, which would be important and elegant in its own right, and the kind of considered, fine room that I like to make for any house.

Textiles are a big part of the Library and a constant point of collecting for me. The patterns of vintage, folk, and simple linens have become the inspiration over the years for carpets, patterns on dishes, and more

products of all kinds. And we use our different linens, casually, every day. It's such an easy thing to invest in a gracious way of living, simply to use cloth napkins or nice dishcloths in the kitchen, among all types of other tablecloths, bedding, and hand towels.

Special textiles and linens hang to air dry. To accommodate these laundering routines, I had the idea to create two niches on either side of the room, which I fitted up with English drying racks. I mounted them

American midcentury plaid and French natural country linens hang on the drying racks.

to the ceiling and painted them like the antique drying rack I've used for years at the Academy, so that they've become a functional part of the architecture. This would be the newer and best version of a place to care for certain things. Every weekend they are filled with washing of some kind.

A laundry room wouldn't be complete without a proper folding table. Central to this special room, I found an antique, red marble stone-topped Chinese table that is high for folding, and beautiful in color and classic form. For different sets of laundry and for transport, I use a collection of the vintage and useful baskets that I always hunt for, in all kinds of ages, sizes, weaves, and colors. Baskets new and old are always a focus in my shopping for Aero and now our shop, Copper Beech. A new style or maker is always a treat. I buy dozens.

The laundry room has two large dryers and one large center washing machine. I quite often encourage clients to have a second dryer to keep the laundry going, so that freshly washed loads don't have to wait. This is a working room, and for this book, flowers spilled over from the potting sink in the next room to this table—a picture to be taken for a book to come.

The 1920s Chinese rosewood table found its place as the center island here; it's just the right height for us. Underneath are a few of the laundry room's French and Belgian baskets, from Aero.

I love the tried-and-true, handsome practicality of the farmhouse sink, with its two compartments and the smartness of the overflow notch between the sides. It comes from a British company called Shaws, which has been making these fine sinks since 1897. And it really is the perfect place for dog washing. The center table is where I give Elcy her haircuts and often arrange flowers, too. The cabinetry is painted in high gloss Moon Mist. The broom is handmade with a natural handle. The classic bee-patterned damask place mats are from Aero.

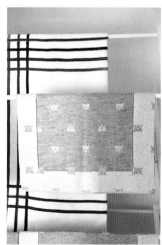

The Wine Room

The wine room at the very bottom of the stairs is in the deepest part of the house where the staircase is a little over three stories tall. On this level and side of the basement are also the root cellar and the cleaning closet, and more built-in closets in the hallway leading to the studio, which are filled with tablecloths and other linens.

Dressers and cupboards are used everywhere in the house for extra storage of different kinds. At the threshold of the wine room is a charming, bleached English oak desk from one of our trips to London, which is the resting spot for many straw hats and garden extras. Then, on one of my working trips to North Carolina for my furniture collections, I came across the charming Black Forest mirror, carved in the shape of a witch. It seemed a funny, bewitching gesture at the bottom of the stairs, as the designator of the spirits in the wine room.

Here in this naturally cool preserve we informally keep cases of wine among more formal furnishings. Sometimes we manage to hold on to champagne for years. This room has become the keeping place for a good portion of my collection of Georgian sprigware vessels and other tobacco jars and pitchers, and among the antique and English things, several pieces of modern photography.

The space is made around some of the more traditional furniture I've designed, which periodically ebbs and flows through the house. Much about the idea of a library honestly did have its first seeds in my

furniture collections. I've always mixed fine Georgian and classical pieces with Continental and modern ones in my client's homes; from those pieces and other antiques that I was saving, I would translate details and forms into my own furniture. By around 2010, I had created a group that I called the Library Collection for

A series of stairs leads to this true little basement level of the house, where the wine room stays cool. At one point there was a thought of putting the oak desk into the master bedroom, but it didn't quite fit and ultimately belonged here much more, with its light pickled wood so nice against the dark floors. Similar to the other furniture in the wine room, I like this unexpected desk with a hat rack above in the basement.

my original furniture partners at Hickory Chair. Several archival pieces from that launch found their way to this Library. They didn't all fit in the furniture plan upstairs but they had a finery and a feeling to them, which became the essence of the wine room.

It was natural to center this low-ceilinged, sequestered, and handsomely dark room around my Riverhouse pedestal table, so that it could be used for resting things as well as tastings and dining—a special destination.

We run downstairs to choose wine and, on occasion, invite guests to have dessert here. The space is meant to be clubby and elegant. I am reminded of my experiences designing restaurants over the years, and even my early days with Ralph Lauren, of all the fun and atmosphere that must go into such rooms if they are to have their own unique character and be a bit free-spirited. These details are so much a part of how I like to design vintage bars and wine rooms for houses.

There are three doors at the bottom of the stairs, to the wine room, the root cellar, and the cleaning closet. Each is fitted with wonderful leftover sample hardware handles from years at the studio, which hadn't ever found their way into projects. These paneled doors here remind me of the charming maze of rooms that one sees in the cellar level of old houses. I had to have them.

My Verona chandelier hangs low over the Riverhouse table in a warm, old tavernlike way, adding to the intimacy and glow of the room. Among the Georgian pitchers on the table are two very fine three-handled loving cups. Other pieces from my Library collection of furniture also hearken back to more classic forms: my Sheffield sideboard is based on a fine George III console table dating to 1785, and the form of a Chippendale case clock. My Acanthus cabinet, which we use here as a chest to store wine as well as dry goods we gather up from our store, Copper Beech, is made with ebony and burled walnut inlay; the richly carved feet are based on an acanthus detail from an elaborate Georgian server.

Around the table is a set of my Emma chairs, from my very first furniture collection. These were based on a trio of shattered, old, painted Chippendale-style chairs that I restored. I've written much about them over the years, but I love that this set has something lighter and modern about them, too, in this dark room, in a pale French Grey finish.

Georgian and now. I am so taken with the amazing detail and finesse in the art of Georgian sprigware. Most of the pieces here come from the wonderful collector who has also helped me so much with my knowledge and selecting of Georgian silverware. Leaning behind one of these pitchers is a favorite photograph of antlers by Michelle Arcila, a gifted artist who once worked for me at Aero. I love her uniquely modern and dreamlike photography.

Spirits and champagne are stored simply among Georgian pitchers and a covered tobacco jar. In this dark room downstairs, an antique chart of the night sky above features both Dan's and my constellations, the lion and the twins; it was a gift to us from our dear friend and writer, Lisa Light, who works on all my books with me.

OPPOSITE: In the autumn we harvest apples from the old apple trees in the gardens. They do find their way into the wine room as well as the root cellar. Also at times, I store flowers here during the week: I bring down vases full from the house and most often they are still beautiful for the next weekend. The center table overflows with branches of black and red raspberries and Wentworth cranberry viburnum. I use the room as my other and most beautiful refrigerator.

Out to the Garden

In the shade and depth of this green place, the Library House is about the romance of the garden in many ways. The special old trees, the discoveries and seasons, and the different garden spaces were all so important to the idea of the house and what I wanted to protect here. One of the first things I dreamed of was a classic European walled garden. On one side of the wall is the sunlit sunken garden, where all the outdoor passages meet. On its other side is the sheltered woodland of the walled garden itself, with the garden house that is hidden at the end of everything.

The Sunken Garden

The garden here is really made up of many separate garden spaces. Each has a different identity and position in the topography around the houses. The Academy and now the Library sit on top of a bluff that rolls down ever so slightly to the water: the village of Bellport is itself essentially without hills or big shifts in landscape. But with that tiny bit of elevation, I wanted the gardens, like the house, to be able to step up and down in the height between spaces. Having a sunken garden was part of that, and a feature I'd always imagined creating here.

The long, terraced steps of the main allée gently bring us down to the lower ground that holds this garden. When we turn the corner to the back of the house, we arrive in a shallow clearing. And this space has so much sun in it—the surprise of an uncovered expanse after the enveloping canopy of the allée and then the towering beauty of the copper beech tree, with the old hinoki cypress in its shade that is the focal point at the end of the view and the beginning of the sunken garden. The garden was planned in this way because I knew what would happen with the light in this open, central spot, especially where the light would travel in the winter, from the initial plantings that I did here before and during the construction. From this resting point, we step back up to the walled garden or up through the large gates by the copper beech to the lawn and pool at the Academy. Views climb along these pathways so that there is a sense of discovery and change along each of them.

ABOVE: The back façade of the library wing. At the end of the narrow attic is a little windowed space with a view to the garden.

PREVIOUS PAGES: The three-hundred year-old copper beech tree stands at the center of the property between the Academy and the Library. It is visible from the Great South Bay.

Sunflowers, lavender, and dahlias fill the planting beds behind the library. The lion-head spout directs water with the gentlest sound into the lead cistern below the window. In the warmer months, plants and pots spill into the center and onto the low steps leading into the walled garden. We have figs and roses, verbena, allspice. Here and across the sunken garden, there have been more herbs in the beds at times. But our dozens and dozens of adorable, ravenous rabbit visitors eat everything. So herbs now can only be grown in the kitchen garden at the Academy, which is protected.

The sunken garden is framed on one side by the lightness of the white-painted and paneled brick façade and the pair of tall doors at the end of the library room, and on the opposite side, by the varied, colorful plantings along the redbrick wall into the next garden. There are five different planting beds here that hold favorites such as roses and lavender, along with peony, asparagus, sunflowers, and dahlias. I do love the beautiful, rustic, low bluestone walls that create the beds in this space. The stones here were all hand-cut and so carefully fitted and finely placed; all the deep, huge slabs that make up the steps to the library and to the other garden spaces were hand-selected for each location.

Most special is the classic garden element of a lead cistern with its lion fountainhead, placed underneath the center window of the library wall that looks into the Georgian cabinet—and, added later, the beautiful antique marble column that we found recently; it is the last formal ornament that we were looking for to complete this space. The sound of the water in the garden is so lovely, especially at night. During our first summer in the house, we planted sunflowers around the fountain and against the garden wall; they will always be a constant here. In the late summer afternoons, the beds are filled with goldfinches feeding on the seeds.

This garden for sitting and sunning holds an array of favorite vintage wrought-iron furniture that I'd saved over the decades. Many years ago I found the pair of striking, dark green chairs with unusual, repeating scrolled details. I've never been quite certain where they come from, and there are many opinions; but all generally agree they date to around 1910. Along with a matched green bench near the copper beech, this favorite set inspired my own collection of garden furniture. Twin nineteenth-century ivory painted scrolled benches sit across from each other, one in front of the greenhouse and the other in front of the cistern. They are from the South of France and are quite uncommon in that they were always kept together as a pair.

The hinoki cypress in the garden. The fine groundcover is made of British hoggin gravel.

We found the beautiful, urn-topped nineteenth-century marble column at one of our favorite antique shops, Theron Ware, in Hudson, New York. We had been hunting for the right, special ornament all along to be the focal point in the central bed between the hinoki and the greenhouse. The column takes the place of an earlier boxwood pyramid topiary that can be seen in some of these pictures.

Casual American and Italian linens and a mix of tableware, old and new. The vintage Swedish Höganäs dishes are part of a set that we often use for simple dining; I love their handsome, earthy green glaze. The ink-blue glasses are my own design for Reed & Barton. I've had the Japanese indigo fan for many years. The hexagon-shaped basket is a favorite for carrying flatware. The Depression glass, green etched pitcher is exactly the same as the one my grandmother had and served lemonade in. I can see it clear as day where she used to store it above her sink.

The Greenhouse

For years, the sunroom at the Academy functioned as a virtual greenhouse, so when the Library was being planned, I wanted to finally build a proper greenhouse to serve all the gardens. Having this one is such a help, centered here in the midst of everything.

It is, in fact, a somewhat odd and conspicuous place for a greenhouse, in such a central part of the garden. Primarily I was inspired by a long-saved image of a vintage English garden with a much older, high brick wall that had a greenhouse attached to one side of it.

At the same time, I needed to find a way to gain approval for a freestanding brick wall so that I could build the walled garden. That image of the English garden gave me the perfect solution: the wall allowed me to have a greenhouse, and the greenhouse allowed me to build the wall, in exactly the charming old way that I had hoped for.

This is a working greenhouse that we use all year-round. It is absolutely full all winter long. A low projection of the wall forms its base with beautiful, scallop-shaped brick coping. I began with a manufactured structure from a wonderful greenhouse builder and added a custom door, painted Litchfield Green. Inside, instead of a traditional dark slate or brick floor, I wanted a different lightness and chose the pale firebrick that I used in all the fireplaces in the house. As the greenhouse leans against the brick wall with the stone frame of the garden wall archway beside it, and all the plants around it, the modern building disappears and ages into the character of a much earlier time.

THIS SPREAD AND PREVIOUS PAGES: The late afternoon sun sets over the greenhouse and the walled garden. In this sunniest spot, the greenhouse catches the light even in winter. In the evenings it becomes a glass lantern in the garden, twinkling among the trees.

Inside the greenhouse is an ever-changing assortment of pots and crocks to hold plants of all kinds. I am forever hunting for unique and special ones, and the group here includes a good deal of both Italian and American pottery.

We found the vintage slate sink in Maine and built a simple cedar base for it; it drains through to the ground right in the center of the garden. The two faucets in the sink are set up to receive hoses. This vintage pair of spigots was part of the early thinking that became my plumbing collection for Waterworks; I'd had them in the studio at Aero for years. Old things that become other products do get a new life in this fortunate way when it's their time.

The Walled Garden

The hidden walled garden is a world here unto itself. With its special old-growth trees, I like to think it has the feeling that it's always been here, long predating the house, but it is new and completely transfigured. This refuge among the trees is the space I always wanted to create surrounding a garden house, as the very last part we come to in the entire garden.

In thinking about the garden so much in the earliest stages of the project, I began with several lovely, particular trees that I'd inherited with the property: a large Kwanzan flowering cherry; an old-growth apple tree; a huge, sprawling English yew; an old, charming dogwood. These trees were growing in this backmost yard behind the previous house; others I added and moved here to tend to them, including a few small

hinoki cypress and seedling apple trees. I really used this area as a bit of a nursery during the intensity of construction, protecting the trees with planted beds in front of them. I knew the trees would become the ingredients of the walled garden here, with more of a woodland and rusticated, ancient feeling than anywhere else around the house.

Then came the idea to create the garden house itself, and to have elegance in the midst of this simple, wild, leafy walled setting. The existing trees were quietly on the diagonal across from each other, which began to create alignment and a frame around a center space. The delicate cherry tree was reserved to one side, where we actually built the end of the brick wall to nestle around it. The yew and dogwood were in the back

There is a path at the end of the oval, with the old Macoun apple tree, the dogwood, and one of the two weeping willows across from one another in the garden.

corner across the old yard from the cherry. I've always loved weeping willow trees in Japanese and American gardens of all kinds, so I brought in two mature, lovely, trailing trees, one first by the side of the garden house, and the following year, another on the far side of the garden, as foils to each other on those opposite ends of the space. With trees occupying these four corners, I then had a breakthrough about how to fill the center. It became obvious to make a simply elegant and perfectly beautiful oval.

I've always loved ovals, and that form here became a wonderful element, with a mossy gravel path traveling around a green. The path would go around to create a view, all the way from the library room and through the open archway in the brick wall, to a fine antique English column in the trees on the farthest side of the garden, with flowering viburnum and other abundant ferns and woodland plants growing around it. Dan had given me an old orchard Macoun apple tree for my birthday one year, and that became the one offset tree in the oval. I had the idea then to plant a soft bed of periwinkle around the tree, like a carpet.

Dan has the charming habit of walking when he talks on the phone, and I have watched him do this often around the pool at the Academy. Part of the reason for the path here was to make him a meditative walking space around the oval. We come out to the little table here in the garden quite often on Sundays for coffee and breakfast with the paper. And we are out here all the time in the late spring through the fall to cook lunch or dinner in the garden house. The dogs love it, too. We call it the walkaround—from the kitchen garden at the Academy out to the front garden, then over to the Library and down the allée, and at last into the walled garden and around the oval.

The goal was to bring existing old trees on the property together with new plantings, in a manner that would feel as if it all had been growing there for a long time. The girls take a turn around the garden in the morning, with June roses blooming all around. The interior of the oval is planted with periwinkle; the exterior has variegated pachysandra and sage intermixed.

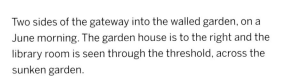

Two sides of the gateway into the walled garden, on a June morning. The garden house is to the right and the library room is seen through the threshold, across the sunken garden.

The architecture in a garden is as important as the plantings. One resource that I have long referred to is a set of quite special garden books by the designer and historian Peter Joel Harrison, filled with all kinds of researched landscape and architectural details. These elegant clothbound volumes are a must for every garden person; I drew inspiration from the books for the precast concrete, limestone-style archway in the brick wall, for the beginnings of the garden shed and the brick paving on the allée, and many trellises that I've made through the years for clients' houses. The idea of the moon window on the far side of the wall then came out of an archetype from classic Chinese gardens.

OPPOSITE: Across the oval. Native woodland angelica covers the foreground near the garden house. Two large cypress trees rise behind the willow. The lush climbing rose along the brick wall was originally trellised on the front of the old house.

ABOVE: We built the brick wall specifically to curve and nest around the cherry tree. The moon window aligns with the second door into the library. Lanterns light the way at the far end of the oval.

The Macoun apple tree rests under the canopy of the willow and the old dogwood tree. We harvest its fruit in the fall. The French chairs and table on the oval came from one of our favorite antique dealers on Lillie Road in London, Victoria Davar and her shop, Maison Artefact. This is where we most often sit in the garden for coffee and breakfast.

OPPOSITE: The end view of the garden is the stone column at the edge of a path into the woodland behind the house. You can see the column on a direct line all the way through the vista from the library room, through the gateway into the walled garden. The little path off the oval is planted with all kinds of textures and colors, including bishop's weed, ferns, nicotiana, and purple-leafed smokebush.

The House at the End of the Garden

In the corner of the walled garden, secreted at the end of the allée, I built a small house with an open-air dining area. From the beginning, this garden house was to be the place with a wood-fired oven and a small interior kitchen, in essence our protected version of an outdoor kitchen for the garden, with a small bathroom and a good deal of storage space with compartments and rooms for all kinds of garden tools.

The inspiration was an image that I'd long had and loved of a 1930s American house with an arched porch. The columns of the arch were squared and shingled and had a very interesting stepped profile to them. I took that idea and made it into a whole house, with a portico of archways on three sides, and shingled columns taken

further with more repeating, stepping profiles. At each corner of the house I made the columns step out even more dramatically; they've become pedestals for a set of pots on the face of the house. Within the portico is the main open-air room, also simply shingled, where we use the oven and have many of our summer and fall meals. The back portion of the house, which holds the kitchen and storage area, follows with a low-slung, cottagelike, gambrel roof.

With the brick wall through to the library view and all the arched details, the little house reminds me of an almost Jeffersonian kind of quiet American elegance. The main brick column of the wood-fired oven is framed by classical, high, stepped pilasters. And to the

The front arched façade of the garden house looks onto the oval. It shelters an open-air room for dining and holds our wood-fired oven. The stepped columns become pedestals for a pair of planted urns. The trellised pergola to the left was built to nestle under the old Kwanzan cherry tree.

side of the house, as you enter the walled garden from the allée, I added an open pergola with trellised panels supported by formal paired columns. So there is this blending of more classic architectural features, just as the walled garden itself is both simple and restful, and at the same time quite composed and delicate.

For the main open room of the garden house, I made a slightly domed tray ceiling with coffered panels. Like other open-air spaces throughout the property, I painted the ceiling panels a classic, soft New England blue. There is a mythology to it in this part of the country, painting outdoor ceilings and porches like the sky to make them look open and keep away ghosts. For the walls, we returned to the idea of yellow that we had originally thought of for the library room, and gave this room that glowing quality. The color is Yellow Bisque by Benjamin Moore.

As much as the garden house contains its New England–cottage and formal Monticello-like ingredients, it was purposeful that these yellow and blue colors, the oval, and the placement in the garden also evoke the warmth and romance of Giverny. As with the design of the main allée, Giverny is an important influence at the Library and a place that Dan and I both so love. The garden house is perhaps the most woven-together French and American mix of any place here.

As in all parts of the garden, we are in and out of the garden house every weekend and during all seasons. We love walking out to the oval and coming into this special space; the view from the archways into the walled garden is one that I return to again and again for inspiration. I will come here to check on everything during the snows of winter, in the lovely silence, when the yellow and blue house is covered in white, waiting for the spring to thaw.

Through the side arch, into the center dining area. The hinoki cypress and the allée follow through beyond. The restful, yellow-painted shingled interior of this space has a resonance of vintage American village life, but it also brings feelings of the French countryside, with such a handsomeness and warmth as you look into it.

Beautiful moss grows amid the natural bluestone that forms walkways around the garden house. Within, the set of wheat back chairs are like the set of chairs that I've always admired in the dining room at Giverny. One Christmas, while the house was under construction, Dan found this set and had the chairs painted yellow to match the walls. We went out that day in the snow to see them in the midst of winter. I always use this pale blue for outdoor ceilings. The doorway leads to the kitchen.

Seeing through. An oval stone pedestal table from Maison Artefact in London stands outside the kitchen; the screen doors extend the view into the woods beyond. I like the soft formality and the classical European details around this open-air room within the walled garden. We both do especially love the French sense of more time spent outdoors, making simple, fresh food, and living at a slower pace. Many weekends, we end up roasting vegetables and fish here in the wood-fired oven.

The interior of the house and its simple cabinetry are clad all the way up to the gambrel roof in fragrant raw cedar. I wanted that charming board-to-board construction that would carry the feeling of an American agricultural building or a rustic lake house. Remnants of the Connemara marble from the Library kitchen came in to create the counters and the top of the vanity in the bathroom. This house is stocked with casual dinnerware, ceramics, and linens, in French blue and yellow colors and patterns.

The two sides of the garden house create different architectural spaces around the open dining pavilion. The trellised side encloses a pergola next to the old cherry tree and the brick wall. It's a quiet place, which I love for its filtered light, to stop off in before going into the garden house. The vintage cast stone birdbath invites visitors amid a set of petite French garden chairs. The kitchen side of the house has a low gambrel roof line in a simple, regional cottage style. In the center is my very favorite, peaceful view into the garden. The mounted lion heads watch over the house; we found them in Petaluma, on one of our trips to Northern California. Just now, as of this writing, a bird has built a nest on top of the lion on the left.

Back to the Studio

This Library House began as a studio and guesthouse and then grew into so much more. With the myriad things that I design, the role of the studio itself evolved into a mirror of the full design office I've always had in the city. It is my study and imagining place for the work of making old things new again that I love to do. Down the open stairs from the library, I draw at my desk in the central, bright studio room, with its own fireside living area. A conference room and all the surrounding resource rooms and cabinets are filled with a complete design library of samples, antiques, and prototypes that I constantly look to for inspiration.

Downstairs from the Library

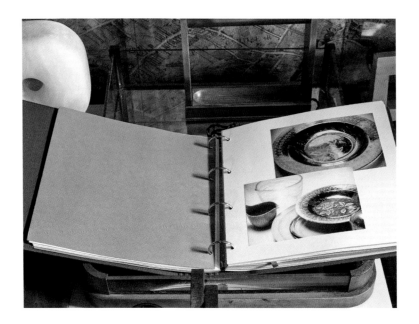

This studio, which was so needed, is numerous things: a chameleon display space; a conference room and set of workspaces; a downstairs great room with its own cooking fireplace and sitting area; a master design archive that holds examples of all the many kinds of items that I have gathered over the decades and which I've made for my store and my home collections. The studio is, both literally and figuratively, the foundation of the whole house.

Of the many spots in the house and garden where we work or study, this is where I do my real designing. I most commonly sit in the main studio room at the same desk table that I made many years ago for my first apartment. I draw here; I pull from all the various collections and samples stored here to assemble ideas for meetings and projects. Downstairs from the library, this large, open room is brightly lit from above and by deep, tall window wells along the side of the house; it is, in a way, the residential version of my design studio in the city, and it's the modern and vintage counterpart to the traditional library upstairs, two connected parts of one continuous story.

On the hearth side of the space, I got to build a special version of a kilnlike cooking fireplace that I'd long admired from the sculptor Brancusi's Montparnasse studio in Paris. It's surrounded by a denlike

ABOVE: I made this early presentation binder around 2002, at the beginning of my collaboration with Marshall Field's. These pages showed concepts for a dinnerware collection, with images of silver luster Wedgwood and modern glass.

PREVIOUS PAGES: The library stairs take us down into the studio. On the stair landing, a collection of ceramics includes hand-thrown bowls from the American South and a neoclassical Copeland platter.

seating area and a large harvest table, where I can sit with clients in and among all the design artifacts. On the allée side of the studio are the conference room and a set of workspaces, lit by bays of windows on the walkway; one such room holds a library unto itself of books and materials from my early days in Soho, including flat files as well many folios of drawings and inspiration books that I've made for various product collections through the years—the kinds of invaluable documents that didn't fit into the bookshelves upstairs.

The studio also includes, of course, designed products of all kinds, in a series of rooms, cabinets, cases, and tables where I've been able to finally assemble the many categories of items that I pull from in all my work. There is a large textile closet with fabrics and linens of every kind; examples of antique and vintage modern lighting, along with previous favorite designs from my past lighting collections; furniture and hardware, both vintage and prototypes; modern Japanese ceramics and glassware, and midcentury American favorites; collections of small objects and table goods; stationery and printworks. There is a time span of what has traveled through two of my studios over the years, in all the things that would be packed up and stored away after a project, brought back here and merged with the personal collections of home wares that I also always worked from. Now it's all together and all visible. And with these elements I can almost change the whole feeling of the studio, depending on the project.

This room, with all the things I'm interested in that I've assembled over time, has become the spot where all of my own time of being a designer has coalesced. That's why it's the studio library it is, because it contains past things and new things that mark where I've been and where I'm going, over these decades of doing what I love.

Parts and pieces, to and for design. On the sill of the window in the conference room. Another presentation book for Marshall Field's shows initial ideas for textiles and bedding. I used pictures of a lovely hotel room with yellow toile on the walls from the first time I'd stayed on the Left Bank in Paris. The images show a collection of my neckties and a blue Vergé de France stationery tablet from G. Lalo on the desk. It has always sat in the middle of my desk at Aero ever since.

The light from the library room flows down the stairs. In the foreground is my working desk where I draw: it's one of the original pair in walnut with vintage aluminum legs that I made years ago for my apartment in New York. A very old pen and ink cabinet, another keepsake antique, holds a collection of Gilles Caffier organic modern French vases, with American and Japanese ceramics and glass. Next to it, at the bottom of the stairs, is my Courtyard table, based on a classical Greek temple table. A poignant image by Sally Mann of her son, Emmett, rests behind it.

A view of the studio, facing toward the conference room. I used the same black marble tile as in the upstairs hallways and designed the floor in quadrants following the ceiling, with different gridded and bordered patterns that help to divide the areas of this large room.

In the way that the house is lifted up to create the tall, lower window wells on the allée, light does flood into the studio all day from the bright window bay. Several areas on this side are set up as different work locations, providing desk space for more designers. To the right is the conference room.

One of the first things that we hung downstairs was the alphabet of charming 1930s calligraphy letters that I found quite by surprise at a churchyard sale in Bellport. Vintage type and lettering of all kinds have always been a fascination for me, and I love teaching tools like this. We used this lettering as the inspiration for the logo of our local store, Copper Beech.

Over a studio desk is an especially large, unique perspective-view map of Paris, dated 1734. Vintage pieces can inspire my new lighting: overhead, my Milton pendant light; on the desk, a number of favorite, individual lamps from my collections for Visual Comfort. Articulating artist chairs for posing sit in front of my whitewashed 1940s Chinese modern cabinet.

Where I work. My Thompson chest holds design resources. Above it, the vintage alphabet begins. On my desk, a deco polar bear is a recurring friend. Above: The Japanese indigo textile is a celebratory symbol of a Madai snapper, which stands for good fortune and happiness; we used it as a logo for our store, Copper Beech. A nineteenth-century plaster copy of *Laocoön* is after the famous sculpture, *Laocoön and His Sons*, in the Vatican. The original design presentation books for my first furniture collection with Hickory Chair are dated November 1998. Three of my older lamps for Visual Comfort sit with a blue glass clock from my first home collection for Target.

To the other side of the room. A large eighteenth-century armoire from northern France holds my collection of hand-painted Italian ceramics and antique transferware. Around a Tennessee farmhouse table, vintage office chairs are covered in shearling. The fireplace is modeled after a European cooking fireplace. In the winters, we will do simple roasting over the coals and have dinner in the studio. A vintage Nakashima chair accompanies a pair of French deco club chairs. My Hicks pendant light hangs throughout the studio, in my favorite combination of bronze and antique brass.

The studio, front to back. At the center of the room is a large Victorian museum case that was such a special find for this house. It serves as a transparent divider between the two sides and the front and back of the studio. The case is filled with vintage lighting treasures and one-of-a-kind things. Behind it, one can see the short set of stairs up to the laundry room.

The conference room is joined with a lower architecture and design workspace. We installed a camera above the table, so that I can draw and share sketches and floor plans with my team in New York. My Patrick pendant light is inspired by a vintage European surgical lamp. At the time of this photo, the conference table was set with a presentation for a new accessory line that I'm designing from many times and cultures. The abstracted photographs of morning dew on spiderwebs are by my friend, artist Laura Resen.

OVERLEAF: Forms and themes. Some of the core inspirations for the new accessory collection are varied stone and marble animal figures, map weights, and tortoise shells: some pre-Columbian and others Chinese, both antique and more ancient.

Going Upstairs

The upstairs of this house is a set of rooms that form a special master suite. This is where family and friends come to stay, and it holds cabinets full of other collections that make up the Library—from worlds traveled in a balcony sitting room at the top of the stairs to the fine furniture and artwork in the master bedroom and its sitting room. Sheltered and restful as it is here, I think the suite is perhaps the prettiest and most delicate part of the house. And at the very end of these rooms, there is a different kind of sanctuary: a glamorous bathroom with all the luxury of 1930s London and vintage American elegance.

The Bedroom Hallways

Creating these guest rooms, along with the studio, had to do with the very earliest idea of what the Library House would be. And it was entirely the cause for imagining a second story of the house that would hold these rooms in a quite private and individual way. We're lifted up here, and the whole floor carries that light spirit in its colors, furnishings, and loveliness among the trees, as the main stairway brings us back to the front of the house. The better part of the floor is itself a suite that sits above the front rooms on the main level. From the stairway, a balcony landing precedes the suite, providing even more of a pause before one finally steps into the master sitting room and bedroom, and at the last, a marble-paneled bathroom.

It's significant that this floor is a library, too, with a different and special kind of fine domestic things that are tucked in throughout these rooms, in chests of drawers and cabinets. This floor also holds its own collection of art as a principal part of the decor. The paintings, etchings, and photographs here are more poetic; most are of a time from one hundred years ago or so. They all have a peaceful feeling.

I especially love one uncommon Eugène Atget photograph, of a rustic French village on the outskirts of Paris. The image has such a romantic yet domestic feeling that captures what I wanted to do in these rooms: find what is casual and timeless in beautiful old things and places.

In my Darby Bowfront Chest, I keep a collection of batiks, table linens, and indigo from Bali and Japan.

PREVIOUS PAGES: A French Louis XV-style armchair in the master suite. In an 1897 Alfred Stieglitz image of Paris, goats rest along the bank of the Seine. Imagine that.

The Balcony Sitting Room
and Bathroom

At the top of the stairs is a small sitting room and guest bathroom, occupying the second balcony that overlooks the kitchen. In spirit it is connected to the two-story height of the great library room, but upstairs it is an intimate, peaceful landing that links the two floors of the house.

As much as the library is settled into the green of the garden, this second floor has a blue and natural feeling that brings us to the spirit of this

house by the sea—to many worlds traveled and a mix of patterns, textiles, and antiques from different cultures. Watching over it all is a large, late 1920s American painting of a sailor that I found years ago. As someone who has always liked and lived with portraits, I appreciate the way that a portrait can become an old friend, a guardian, who gives his or her personality to a room. This nautical character fit the balcony in particular.

Equally important is the pair of very large, Italian terra-cotta eagles that I found at an auction in London. I knew from their size that they would be magical and protective here, with one positioned to watch over the

balcony and the kitchen below, and the other facing into the landing. The eagles are a dramatic surprise that might be more likely to be placed formally paired. I was inclined to use them in a more casual way, counting on their elegance to give the balcony its special character. The eagles live up in this lofty place.

The landing also provides an extra guest bathroom. I designed it in a classic 1930s, British deco style, as a partner to the marbled master bathroom farther into the main suite. The idea for this space came from a favorite image of an English bathroom that had a mirror-fronted tub with bronze rosette mounts to hold the glass. I used this simple detail here and on the mirrored wall over the sink. The room is essentially made up of a set of panels, each different on each elevation, holding mirror, marble, or wood. The same Greek marble used in Dan's office bathroom vanity downstairs makes the panels around the bathtub, as well as forming the casing around the window. Another vintage ingredient in this room that I often use in design projects is the very glossy, hardy white paint, bright and crisp and so reflective and European.

A Japanese nautical plaque rests with two of a graduated set of three very large English papier-mâché trays. The balcony provides a closer view of the French Impressionist landscape painting that hangs high in the kitchen. A comfortable wing chair for reading was a London find. I've kept the cobalt blue glass vase from my grandmother O'Brien since my first college apartment days.

OVERLEAF: The balcony. A handsome Stickley oak library table holds the terra-cotta eagles. The doorway at the end of the hall is to the bathroom. The American sailor painting is from the 1920s.

We found the handworked old needlepoint camelback sofa on one of our trips to Northern California. Pillows and throws are made of American tattersall, madras cloth, and fabric from Panama. Some things here are rustic and handcrafted, others are more refined. It's color and varied culture that bring these things from so many places together, on the rich needlepoint.

The small midcentury compass table was found on Lillie Road in London. I love the charm and intricacy of all its multi-directional points, and how the table is something a little more modern in the midst of all the antiques. The book of knots has such an elegant, graphic cover; it was meant to be with the table in this space that is about seagoing.

Marble and millwork. Each wall in the bathroom is a variation of a raised panel: the tub and shower marble are contained by paneled moulding and each wall is another paneled moulding variation. The details of mirror, marble, and paneling, and even the classic glass rod towel bars, evoke vintage deco bathrooms, but with a freshness and brightness for now.

The Master Sitting Room

Of all the upstairs spaces, and really all the decoration at the Library, the master sitting room is the prettiest and likely the most antique room we have in this house. The darker nautical blues of the balcony sitting room transform and subdue into a more ethereal, pale, patterned and gilded softness, along with the sheerest of the grey paint colors in the house that becomes the primary shade of the doors throughout the master suite, the aptly named Cumulus Cloud. This room is something of a symbolic pair with my office off of the library room: both are primarily floral and quite classical, appointed with fine furniture and graceful treasures.

The first key to the room was the lovely fluted and columned antique mantelpiece: I bought it at least ten years ago for its perfect carving and slender proportions and had stored it for safekeeping in the garage next door at the Academy. Even with its chalky finish and Doric refinement, it always reminded me of the living room fireplace in my first little cottage in Brookhaven, New York. In certain ways, this sitting room is a re-creation of that special, antique, diminutive, and so-comfortable living room.

The mantelpiece's fluting and classicism made a strong connection to another long-saved piece of furniture that immediately belonged here: an incredibly elegant, gorgeous, reeded early nineteenth-century Danish secretary that I found years ago but can never

remember where from, auction or shop. It has been a beauty stored away for so long, one of those rare and exceptional pieces that I periodically find ages before I have any place for it. It was waiting to find its home. It felt absolutely made for the very front corner of this gracious room, and of the whole house in a sense, glowing in the light of the windows onto the front yard. I've long wanted to adapt and make this secretary; now that it is here and during the process of writing this book, it is at last being considered to be reinterpreted and produced for my Century Furniture Collection.

As the first room of the enfilade that makes up the master suite, the sitting room sits directly over Dan's office and shares the same natural, dreamlike, corner light. That light helped point me to the floral elements of the furnishing that would feel so beautiful and sensual in this environment. The many layers and elements of pattern in the room add to a tranquility, which was what I wanted most for this space. From all the way back in my first days at Ralph Lauren, I had saved the very traditional polished chintz that covers the pair of English armchairs; I had never quite found the place I wanted to use it, and when I finally chose the chintz for these chairs, I had just enough to upholster them both. The printed cotton drapery fabric, though new, was likewise soft and evocative of vintage European sitting rooms in grey, ivory, and blue: they are the first

On the fluted mantelpiece, a pair of lovely amethyst birds on gilded bases nests among vintage forest photographs. Everything here has a delicacy and a luminous fineness that is wonderfully calm.

and only printed drapes in the house, and they continue on into the master bedroom. My Corsaro rug in ocean blue-green was the very thing to add a somewhat airier pattern of floral medallions to the floor in an extension of the room's palette.

Other furniture here has that most elegant, slightly perishing and well-used quality of antique rooms that I admire. The very fine painted Swedish chair is another true beauty, with its original peach silk cushion and tassels that are worn and aged, so charmingly and casually laced around the legs. I was able to bring back my favorite soft linen-covered sofa from my old

Brookhaven house that is still so plush and comfortable when one sinks into the stuffed down cushions.

But what most connects all the pieces in this room is the art. Above the sofa is a gallery-hung grouping of intricately patterned drawings and etchings. In their center is an antique panel painting mysteriously called *The Swamp*, which fit just exactly inside a rare, 1940s English modernist frame with the red clay undercoat showing through the age-worn gilding. This is the one spot in the house with such a gallery wall character—a favorite way to reflect on how things relate to one another.

One of the amethyst birds perches on a book that I so love for the elegance of its title: *The Opal Sea*. A vintage black-and-white Tina Modotti photograph stands next to it. On the gallery-hung wall across the room, I brought together abstractions: tiny drawings and an intricate Japanese screen for printing kimono fabrics, alongside an expressionist painting.

A Gilded Age. An American silver gilt oval mirror had the right elegance for this delicate, fluted mantelpiece. The French art deco, patinated bronze sconces frame the oval form. In the center of the mantel is a superb gilded box, so purely classic and refined, that was a favorite find from one trip to London.

I still love the simplicity of the sofa from my original little house at the beach, paired with the chintz chairs covered for this room. The later modern, bleached mahogany coffee table with a pale green leather top, from California, is part of the mix of traditional and modern that Dan and I are always looking at.

A fine Spode dish sits on a fretwork table that had been stored in the attic at the Academy. The dish was an early purchase on one of my very first trips to London with Ralph Lauren in the late 1980s. The blue-glazed lamp is Chinese and the cast iron dragonflies are from Japan. I am always inspired by the naturalism and extraordinary craft of objects from the East. The very beautiful Danish secretary sits in the calming, all-day northern light of this corner of the house. I always knew it was meant to go right here. With the chintz, the drapes, the china, and so many other ornamental things, this became the pretty room that they could finally all be in.

Leaning on the top of the secretary is a 1797 Italian map of the east coast of North America, by the cartographer Cassini. It is paired with a late-period Egyptian basalt head, pieces of Murano glass, and another 1920s Tina Modotti photograph. The desk holds an exquisitely produced scrapbook of photographs by Jacques Henri Lartigue, published in 1966. The very fine painted Swedish chair is eighteenth-century Gustavian, with a beautifully carved back panel depicting an elaborate urn with foliage and drapery.

The Master Bedroom

The sequence of rooms that make up this master suite is much like the group of connected rooms that I reconfigured to form the master suite of the Academy. I did have this relationship in mind as I was creating the design of these spaces. The transitions here make a set of visual chapters in a way, as we move from the floral, lovely blue sitting room into the middle room, this master bedroom, with its handsome, classical silhouettes against the surprise of pale pink walls. And from the bedroom the movement continues to the stronger dark and light contrast of the dramatic marble bathroom.

This bedroom began, as many rooms do, with a carpet. I discovered this rare, exceptional nineteenth-century Chinese Ningxia dragon carpet at auction; I fell in love with the elongated, scrolling dragons and geometric fretwork border, and especially its very unusual coloring, with darkest chocolaty-purple figures on an ivory background. It fit so exactly in this space, like magic, when we laid it down for the first time. The elegant color of it was the reason for the choice of the delicate Tissue Pink paint for the walls of the room.

I'd originally designed my Stanford bed as a custom commission for a client. To me, the pink of the walls with the bed's rich, modern Georgian woodwork creates a tailored character, much like a pale pink shirt under a dark suit; and this relates to the soft blues in

Pink walls balance the strong silhouettes of the bed and the dragon carpet. Hanging above is a favorite Milton Avery pastel of a woodland riverbed, from 1942. A pair of my Gallia stools in pickled oak with bone leather combines with the pale pink and blue airiness of the bedding to soften the palette of the room.

the sitting room as well. I have often used pale peach and pink colors in bedrooms for their soothing, flattering qualities, and we have since used the Tissue Pink in Dan's and my offices in our studio in the city. It is a very nice connection for us between town and country.

In this room of powerful silhouettes, I'd also found the large and striking Venetian table at a furniture gallery in Tennessee: I knew it was to be the library table here, set against the front windows, another defining placement in the early plans of the house. Though newly made, it is beautifully crafted with a hexagonal wood tabletop, classically Venetian in style.

Certainly the table forms a relationship with the bed across the room, along with the very fine, early modern, 1920s Swedish cabinet. This piece has such sensitive and intricate inlay, a companion in elegance and classicism to the Danish secretary next door in the sitting room. In this room, and others like it that I design for clients, I do like emphasizing how very pretty and formal things can still be strong and bold: the combination of soft color and rich wood, silhouette and detail, creates not only balance but also a refined order.

That's completely true of the ivory-colored French Louis XV–style armchairs in this suite, which we discovered by chance, covered in precious leopard silk velvet—a material that is so dear and meticulously handcrafted, which I've admired for years and always looked to use in the most special places. Dan and I found the set of four chairs walking through Christie's one year just before our anniversary and thought hopefully to buy them for each other. We put in a bid, not really expecting to win them, but good fortune was with us. They are now called our anniversary chairs. They add a kind of gentle Parisian feeling in this bedroom, on this entire floor of blended cultures and collections.

Above one of the French Louis XV chairs, a carved foliate deco lamp lights the corner of the room. Across the Venetian table, the very beautiful, inlaid Swedish cabinet fills the wall shared with the sitting room.

My Darcy silk-shaded double hanging light is positioned with the large Venetian writing table at the center of the room. Embroidered South American belts sit with Italian goatskin gloves. The orange dressing set is Bauhaus, an important treasure from the earliest days of Aero.

THIS PAGE AND OVERLEAF: Two views of the bedroom. In the enfilade of the master suite, the bedroom provides a framed view of the bathroom. The mirrored doors on the left enclose a closet; a dressing room is to the right. The doors in the hallway are paneled with mirror on both sides so that open or closed, they reflect light into the vestibule between the bedroom and bath.

In the other direction, the colorful and floral sitting room is visible beyond the pale pink bedroom. On the bed, the duvet is made of my Davis Stripe damask, topped with an ivory goatskin fur coverlet. The cabinet is Swedish from the 1920s, designed by Carl Malmsten, and made in Macassar ebony with classical marquetry inlay. I found the English armchair in a shop in Southampton, and it was the last, missing piece that the room needed.

The mirrored dressing room hall and dressing room hold a collection of modern black-and-white photography   works by Doug Inglish, Gary Schneider, Edward Curtis, and others. On my Tricia chest is a Bruce Weber portrait photograph from his series "Chop Suey Club." The mahogany Chinese dressing mirror is from the wonderful Los Angeles shop Blackman Cruz. My crystal-block Ryan puzzle lamp is from my earliest Visual Comfort collection.

The Master Bath

I will never forget my first trips to London in the late 1980s, working for Ralph Lauren, when I stayed at the famous Claridge's hotel for the first time, and really saw how a legendary bathroom was made and outfitted. In all the interior styles that we as designers can work in, for bathrooms I still believe nothing surpasses the perfect material elegance and mix of form and function in the golden age of fine baths and spas of the 1920s and 1930s. The skilled panelizing of marble and sparkling grids of mosaic and tile; the languorous spaciousness, like living quarters; the attention to every bit of fitted metalwork detail; the question of what in a bathroom is made of stone and what parts provide the relief where there isn't stone: these forms intrigued me, and I learned from them. I still use those lessons today.

This space is made in that remembered style of English deco sophistication that impacted me all those years ago. One of the first choices was the dramatic, highly veined Calacatta Paonazzo marble that I'd originally selected for the kitchen, which lent itself to a light-to-dark, white, grey, and black-accented room. Another choice was the fireplace, which is the endpoint of the view all the way through the master suite from the sitting room: additionally, it divides the bathtub side of the room from the shower and vanity on the other. With this fireplace, in this paneled marble room, I knew I wanted another dark painting like the ones in the front entrance hall. I had this magical 1925 Impressionist nocturne scene of New York City that I once hung in the conference room at Aero, just the right picture and the right period. Now in a wonderful combed gilded frame, it is this evocation of Jazz Age city glamour, full of life.

Many of the other elements of the room are about a precision of shaping and fitting that I love to detail in stone and metalwork. The cabinetry and marblework of the vanity have faceted, clipped corners in a deco style, based on the bath in that first hotel room I stayed in at Claridge's. All of the marble—in the shower, behind the bathtub and vanity, around all the windows—is carefully panelized like millwork. The nickel-plated frame of the shower turns the corner and creates a glass box on two sides, where the two planes of light, not one, make all the difference. My Venice sconces in the room are special convex, silvered orbs that I designed based on an antique convex mirror in a square wood frame. Each of these elements is really quite simple, geometric, and crisp on its own: this bathroom is about loving materials, and scaling and interpreting the purest of forms in the most elegant and lavish ways.

Dark into light. The bathroom glows in white, cream, and grey with black and ebony details. My black ceramic Chloe lamp is graphic and sculptural on a leather-topped table of my design, with white peonies from the garden. The central fireplace is given a strong silhouette with an ebonized and burled wood Dutch frame profile. The paw-footed low footstool is a quite rare piece by T. H. Robsjohn-Gibbings. The nocturne painting is likely in New York City and from the 1920s.

THIS PAGE AND OVERLEAF: A very fine Robsjohn-Gibbings klismos chair, along with the paw-foot stool, were specially commissioned and made for a Dayton's department store display window in Minneapolis in the 1970s. I loved the connection to my history, as Dayton's was the parent of Target in that exact location. On the other side of the fireplace is the panelized marble shower and the deco-inspired vanity. I designed my Venice sconces for this room during the construction of the house. The green linen damask towels were found on an afternoon wandering in Venice. These towels are always kept here . . . always the green of the garden.

At the end of all these efforts, in literally the last room we come to in the whole of this house, I got to make that kind of space that I'd always dreamed of having. It's an honor to work in an aesthetic that touches the spirit of another time, where my job is to know the ingredients well and make something of them that is authentic. The hope in all that I do is to create things that have a substance and a memory, that carry something of a past and feel that they will last into a future. It's the before, the now, the after. Design for me is about making the things worth keeping, that will carry on traditions I love and respect for a long time to come.

Acknowledgments

I've always believed that homes are the best expression of where we've been and where we're going. The fruits of that journey are everywhere in this house, in all the things and ideas I've brought together over time. But I did not do it alone. This house also holds the shared fruits of the labor of so many wonderful people who have been part of making the Library with me.

First among these is my remarkable husband, Dan Fink. We have done this together and our life here keeps me going. All that I have loved and think of, all that I imagined this to be, is for you. Our house holds what lasts and what lies ahead. And for me, that is always you.

I would like to thank the dedicated people who had a hand in designing and constructing the house and garden. Sebastian Lebski is my creative director and lead architect. We've worked together for many years and he saw this whole house through, with such constant talent for finding the correctness of each element. Aaron Rigby was an early contributor to the architecture, and he made the beautiful hand drawings of the property and gardens that have become the book's endpapers.

The house was beautifully built with pride and great craft by Koral Brothers builders from Southampton, led by Steve Napoli. One of the best things about the project was discovering our friend and highly skilled carpenter, Roger Roldan. Roger shaped each detail with such knowledge, love, and care. He turned the same care toward building our store, Copper Beech. Onward we go, with many projects ahead.

Suvi Asch is my skilled gardener and horticulturalist, an invaluable partner who brings such a sensitivity to her work. My trusted landscape contractor and friend Matt Palermo has done exceptional work here. Arborist Joe Wruck has been with me the longest of this team, taking artful care of all the trees here. Without them the gardens would not have all the nurtured magic that they do.

I've known Allen Gross now for nearly thirty years and together we have been through many large projects, including moving and building Aero three times. He, along with Terri Cannon-Nelson, persevered in the business orchestration of this most complex project, and kept it all going. This house would never have been built without their imaginative help.

At Aero, Kevin Mejia is one of the hardest working people I've ever met. I entrust him above all others to transport and care for every object, including these years of collecting that had to be considered and sorted through as they were moved to the Library. Special thanks to Keith Kancar, who stays with me, steadies the course, and has seen what this house could become for our partners and our work together. Matthew de Clementi is my exquisitely talented Aero store manager. Time and again I've turned to him for everything from Aero, old and new, and for his so-careful and knowledgeable help. My thanks to all the Aero staff present and past, for their support and contributions through the years.

I'm proud to make my books with Abrams, such a rare, special, and distinguished publisher. Deepest thanks to my editor Rebecca Kaplan, for her fortitude and vision. She always supported the idea of making this book as I saw it, this story of a walk through the house and the way it shares my life. I'm so happy that Miko McGinty returned to us for the design of this book after collaborating on my first book, *American Modern*, in such a refined and informed way.

I met Francesco Lagnese on a photo shoot of the Library for *Veranda* magazine. I was immediately impressed, not just by the beauty of his pictures, but also the way he makes them. Beyond his talent and craft, he is such a lovely and charming man. Thank you for creating the portrait of how the house really feels that I so hoped for. My thanks to Michelle Arcila for her friendship and for capturing luminous images of the garden and the house that we added to the book.

To my generous friend and writer, Lisa Light. This is our third book together, and so much that's in it is part of our long history and all you've written about everything I make. You know better than anyone how personal the making of this house has been. Thank you for your patience and your delicate art and language as we figured together how to tell the story of the Library, over many years.

In this house full of art, particular thanks is due to my trusted framer Russ Gerlach, who took his work to such a special level for so many elements here. I so admire Alpaslan Basdogan at Asia Minor Carpets, for his eye and his creativity, and for how he manages to make such beautiful things in a changing world. I always turn to my favorite Theron Ware in Hudson, New York, to Joel Mathieson, and to all the lovely shops on Lillie Road in London. To quintessential dealers like Mr. Devenish and Roger Warner and all the others who now bravely try to have shops: you keep the faith of finding beautiful things and bringing them forward.

The end of these pages lies in a lucky beginning. I would not be the person or the designer that I am without my grandmother, Dellamae Betts Wickwire. I like to think that she would be so proud of me for what the gardens here are and what the house is made to be. From her I learned to take pride and industry in the making of a home, to tend to what one cares about, with joy, day in and day out. That's how I feel about my life here with Dan and all of what I try to do and make.

So, this book is also for Dellamae, who took my hand and walked me to the library in her own New York village, time and time again, and taught me so much about looking at the world and what was beautiful and why.

EDITOR: Rebecca Kaplan
DESIGNER: Miko McGinty
PRODUCTION MANAGER: Rebecca Westall

Library of Congress Control Number: 2017956869

ISBN: 978-1-4197-3261-4
eISBN: 978-1-68335-333-1

Printed and bound in United States
10 9 8 7 6 5 4 3 2 1

ABRAMS The Art of Books
195 Broadway, New York, NY 10007
abramsbooks.com

Poolhouse

Garden House

Walled Garden

Cherry

Fireplace

Pool

The Copper Beech

Sunken Garden

lawn

Lily of the Valley

Portico

Kitchen Garden

Garage

Locus Allee

Screen Porch

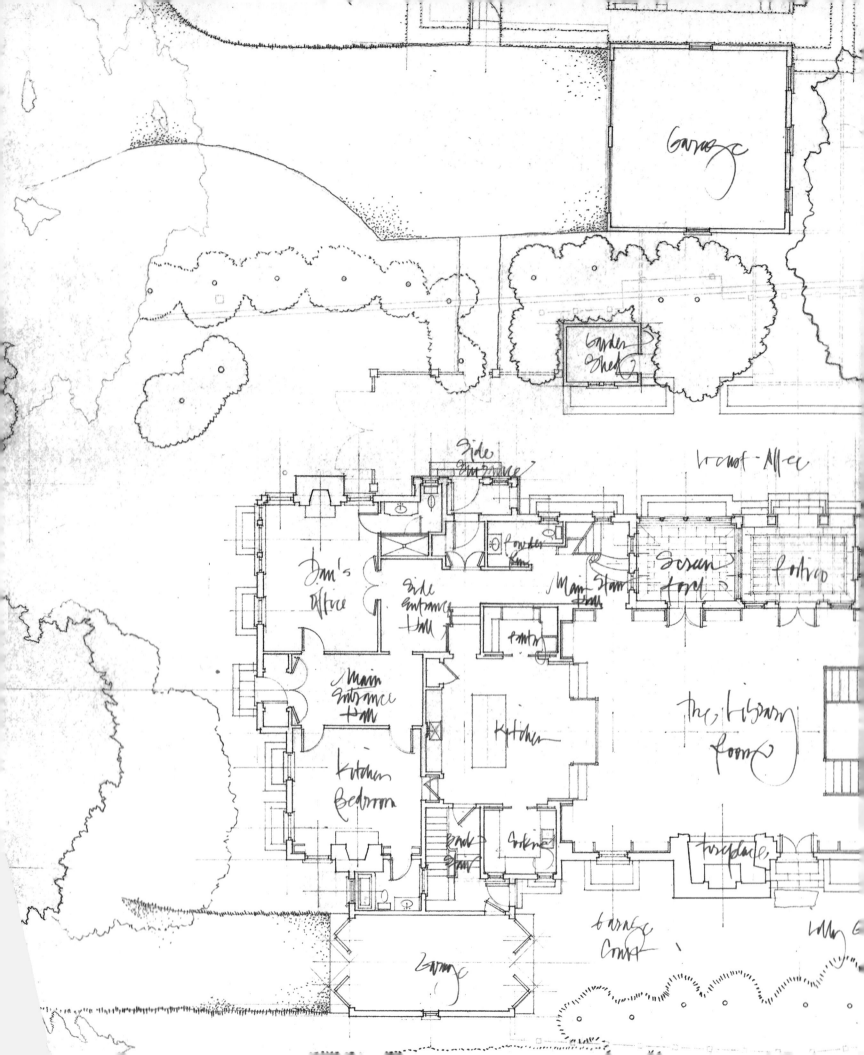

Garage

Garden Shed

Side Entrance

Dan's Office

Side Entrance Hall

Main Entrance Hall

Kitchen Bedroom

Kitchen

Powder Rm

Main Stair Hall

Pantry

Screen Porch

Portico

the Library Room

Back Stair

Cooking

Fireplace

Garage Court

Garage